THEY NEVER SAW IT COMING ...

An Employer's Guide for
Reducing Stress and Violence in the Workplace

Robert F. Conte
Attorney & Counselor

THEY NEVER SAW IT COMING...

by Robert F. Conte, Attorney & Counselor

Cover design by:
Alphagraphics®
South Bend, Indiana

Library of Congress Catalog Card Number

2003113545

ISBN 1-879183-61-7 (Paperback)

Copyright © 2003 by Robert F. Conte

ALL RIGHTS RESERVED

Printed in the United States of America

Bristol Banner Books
14041 C.R. 8
Middlebury, IN   46540
USA

PREFACE

MY PURPOSE IN WRITING THIS BOOK

"We make a living by what we get; we make a life by what we give."

--W. A. Nance

This book represents an accumulation of many professional experiences combined with an understanding of the numerous problems and laws that impact the workplace on a daily basis. Through years of counseling employers in the seemingly endless task of trying to create an employee-friendly work environment and by helping employers manage diversity, through the introduction of honesty, integrity, compassion and respect, positive results have occurred. Through the development of programs that encourage open communication and teamwork, we found that workplace harmony was improved and employees were made to feel that they are an integral part of the organization. Reductions in absenteeism, employee turnover, workplace injuries and the lessening of job-related stresses associated with demands for higher quality, productivity and service are the goals we seek to achieve. The stress that is associated with the workplace is reduced, resulting in the likelihood of reduced anger and violence.

It is my hope that this book will provide guidelines that will assist the employer by planting that single seed, idea or suggestion that will help his business become more successful in the development of an effective employee relations program. While we may not always win the battle, we must always place ourselves in a position to be a positive force in making a difference that will ultimately lead to winning the war.

ACKNOWLEDGMENTS

"Once you have accepted yourself, it's so much easier to accept other people and their points of view."
                                                    --Anonymous

I am deeply indebted to my family who supported me through the many difficult and frustrating periods while writing this book and developing a successful law practice. Their encouragement helped me "carry the day".

To those whose lives have changed due to senseless acts of violence in the workplace.

To my wife Lauren, who painstakingly read and edited the manuscript and helped improve the message.

To my daughter, Deborah Meister and friend Carl Magel, for their insightful comments on the text.

To AnnMarie Ferris, a dear friend, who battled the latter stages of pregnancy and my hand- writing to type seemingly endless pages of the manuscript and its many revisions.

To John M. Morgan, Ph.D., D.Sc., noted author and retired publisher for his "words of wisdom" and encouragement to write this book.

To my good friend and coffee buddy, Lisa Greco, for her insightful comments and endless ideas about sales and marketing techniques.

To Pat Welch and Jon Harmon at Alphagraphics for their ideas and suggestions in designing an "eye-appealing" cover.

To the many authors who preceded me with their writings on the subject of workplace violence. Your thoughts were insightful in understanding the depth of the problem.

Finally, to anyone I may have missed, your omission was unintended. Thank you all!

INTRODUCTION

*"The problem with predicting workplace violence is the
unpredictability of human behavior."*
--Brian L. McDermott, Esq.,
cited in *Violence in the Workplace: An Unfortunate Reality*

Workplace violence has become a nightmare for many
organizations, both domestic and foreign. It is a problem that
has increased significantly in recent years and is now the
fastest growing type of homicide in the United States. Its
long term impact, both financially and psychologically, can
be devastating, affecting families, co-workers and friends.

There have been numerous examples cited over the years
of incidents where violence in the workplace has resulted in
tragic consequences. Incidents in Northern Indiana, in
December 2001, at Nu-Wood Decorative Millwork (Goshen,
Indiana), Bertrand Products (South Bend, Indiana) in March
2002, and Lockheed Martin (Meridian, Mississippi) in July
2003, are illustrative of the problems that can occur when the
stresses caused by our environment turn into rage and then
violence. Generally, the signs that precede these horrible
events go unnoticed or are ignored.

In the Nu-Wood incident, a disgruntled employee shot and
killed the plant's general manager and wounded six other
individuals before taking his own life. At Lockheed Martin,
five people were killed and nine wounded before the disgruntled worker turned the gun on himself, committing suicide.
The Bertrand Products incident was equally tragic. In each
case, the incident affected many people, including the

workers and the community, and the scars remain. These examples are representative of the numerous cases that make up the threat we have come to know as workplace violence.

Incidents of workplace violence are usually followed by countless meetings involving business owners, community leaders, human resources specialists, lawyers and members of management. There are often seminars, newspaper articles, media reports and speeches from various "experts" who center on these tragedies, discuss reasons why they occurred and attempt to develop an awareness of the serious nature of the problem. The result - organizations react by developing policies and prevention programs and then put them into place.

The memories of these tragic incidents linger well beyond the event. While we all wish that these events would have never occurred, the reality is that they did and it can happen anywhere. Can they be prevented? No one has that answer and likely never will. However, in every instance of workplace violence, there are signs that go unnoticed and are often missed. So the scars from these tragic events linger and the healing process, both physical and mental, will likely be everlasting. The thought that it can (and will) happen again is frightening. So the question as to how we might "fix" the problem remains.

This book will look at the many aspects associated with stress and violence and how it affects the workplace. In dealing with the reality of workplace violence, we must recognize that despite our best efforts and intentions, we will not eliminate it from occurring. But maybe, just maybe, hidden within the pages of this book, there is an idea or suggestion that will lead to the prevention of an incident of workplace violence. If that happens, I will have achieved my purpose.

TABLE OF CONTENTS

CHAPTER ONE

DEFINING THIS THING CALLED
WORKPLACE VIOLENCE
"There is nothing we cannot live down, rise above and overcome."

--Ella Wheeler Wilcox

The Problem
"Nobuddy every fergits where he buried a hatchet."

--Kin Hubbard

The world is full of violence. We hear and read about it everyday. While it always seems to be at some distant place, it really is in our presence daily. Whether in the home, at school, or in the workplace, violence has become a growing concern that can no longer be ignored.

The National Institute for Occupational Safety and Health (NIOSH) reports that an average of 20 workers are murdered each week in the United States. Homicide has become the third highest work-related cause of death and has become the leading cause of workplace death among females. Men, however, are at a three times higher risk of becoming victims of workplace violence than women. Statistically, homicide is also the leading cause of death for workers under 18 years of age. In a study conducted from 1980 to 1988, NIOSH released statistics that should be of concern to everyone. This study found that homicide accounted for 12% of all job-related deaths. A very alarming statistic.

The U.S. Bureau of Labor Statistics (BLS), in an independent study, confirmed the NIOSH findings and reported that homicide was the leading cause of death for women at work, accounting for 42% of on-the-job fatalities.

Additional Facts About Workplace Violence
"You can never find yourself until you face the truth."
                                        --Pearl Bailey

- Premeditated workplace violence develops over time.
- Workplace violence includes any verbal and physical assault, or any violence that occurs in the workplace, even if its source is unrelated to the work environment. Suicide is also included.
- Violence in the workplace can also be intruder-initiated when brought about by a non-employee. Domestic violence is a leading factor of such third party actions.
- An employee's use of drugs and alcohol results in ineffectiveness at work, thereby increasing the likelihood of a violent act occurring.
- Workplace violence leads to increased medical and stress related disability claims, lower productivity and higher turnover.
- Violence just does not happen and there is often a triggering event.
- The carry-over effect of violence and harassment affects the health and productivity of everyone. Victims are often left angry, fearful, stressed and depressed (psychological trauma of the event).
- Job stress can be both a cause and an effect of workplace violence. Stress is also a leading contributor to the employee burnout rate.

- Most employers are unprepared to deal with workplace violence. Very little progress has been made over the years: 10% have active programs; 40% have programs, but do little or nothing; 50% have no programs. The employer's failure to act creates a situation whereby employees are placed in danger and an employer's exposure to liability is increased.

Open communication between management and employees are a necessary ingredient that can lower levels of violence and harassment in the workplace. A Zero Tolerance Workplace Violence Policy is a must for every employer.

It can't happen here - Wrong! It can happen anywhere.

What is most alarming about the reported figures on workplace violence is that they fail to include the high number of incidents that do not result in fatalities. The incidents of violence related to physical or sexual assault, which injure but do not kill and acts of sabotage against equipment, materials or property, often go unreported.

Another unreported statistic relates to psychological and/or verbal abuse often associated with workplace violence. Acts such as threats, sexual abuse, demeaning or belittling statements and ridicule are also excluded from the reported statistics. While these acts do not cause direct bodily harm, they can affect an employee's mental health and in turn negatively impact an employer's profitability and overall business health.

Depending on whose figures you choose to believe, the losses resulting from workplace/ domestic violence to U.S. companies both financially and otherwise, are staggering. The following numbers have been reported:

- $4.2 billion per year in lost work and legal expenses. These costs often show up as decreased hours on the job, increased health costs, higher turnover rates and lower productivity on the job. (Bureau of National Affairs, 1990)
- There were 22,400 attacks in the workplace where employees survived but were seriously injured and 1,063 workplace deaths. (Bureau of Labor Statistics, 1992)
- 2.2 million employees were attacked in the workplace, another 6.3 million employees were threatened with violence and still another 16.1 million employees harassed in some way while in the workplace setting. (National Life Insurance Company, 1993)
- The South Bend Tribune on December 9, 2002 cited a National Crime Victimization Survey which reported a yearly loss of 2.8 million work days or $192 million dollars, one-half of which is absorbed by the employer.

While the numbers are staggering, death or injury to an individual should not be an inevitable result of one's chosen occupation, nor should these reported figures be routinely accepted as the cost of doing business in our society. We can no longer ignore the obvious. Something must be done and it must be done now. The problem is not going to go away unless we begin to take action.

Whatever statistic you choose to believe, the numbers are frightening. Clearly, there has been a dramatic increase in the incidents of workplace violence. More alarming is the fact that no definitive strategy exists or has been developed to prevent violence in the workplace. What we have learned is that we need to change the way work is done in an effort to minimize and reduce the risk of injury or death to American workers. Employers and employees alike must begin the process of assessing the risks of violence in their workplace and take appropriate action to reduce that risk. Collecting information about all incidents of workplace violence is a critical first step that will help determine when prevention strategies are necessary, appropriate and effective. Throughout the assessment process, it is important to keep in mind that there are no state-of-the-art security systems, psychological experiences or human resources information that can guarantee an end to workplace violence. However, I am convinced that by taking preventive measures we will help reduce the risk. This book is intended to create an awareness of the seriousness of the problem and to develop ideas that may result in the reduction of workplace violence incidents.

The reader is asked to keep one simple premise in the forefront of their thinking. If you believe it cannot happen in your workplace - you are wrong! Workplace violence can happen anywhere and at any time. In big or small cities, large or small businesses, colleges, schools, hospitals, nursing homes, "mom and pop shops", the list is endless. The problem is real and finding the elusive cure is the responsibility of everyone. It is only through concern, alertness to the problem and the acceptance of the responsibility to do something about it that prevention can effectively take place.

Defining the Problem

"Revenge is a kind of wild justice; which the more man's nature runs to, the more ought law to weed it out."

--Francis Bacon

Workplace violence has many definitions, none of which are pleasant. It has clearly become a phenomenon of the last 25 years, growing in ugly intensity over the last decade. Workplace violence can be described as follows:

- Violence or the threat of violence against workers.
- Any language or action that makes one person uncomfortable in the workplace.
- Any verbal or physical assault that occurs in the workplace including threats and harassment.

In any proposed definition of this subject, bodily injury
inflicted by one person to another is included. Any expansive
definition usually encompasses the entire spectrum of violent
type actions, from offensive language to homicide. Maybe a
more comprehensive definition would be: Workplace
violence is violent acts, including assaults and threats of
assault, directed toward persons at work or on duty.
Violence can occur in or outside the workplace and can
range from threats and verbal abuse to physical assaults and
homicide. Often referred to as a form of "national terrorism,"
workplace violence has become a recurring nightmare for
employers and employees alike. According to NIOSH,
examples of violence include:

Threats: Expressions of intent to cause harm, including
verbal threats, threatening body language and written
threats.

Physical Assaults: Attacks ranging from slapping and
beating to rape, homicide and the use of weapons such
as firearms, bombs or knives. Guns seem to be the
weapon of choice because they are the fastest and most
accessible way to gain a feeling of instant superiority.
It has been reported that guns account for 75% of
workplace homicide deaths.

Muggings: Aggravated assaults, usually conducted by
surprise and with intent to rob.

While violence in the workplace poses a threat to everyone, there are certain situations that may increase the risk of violence occurring, such as interacting with the public, exchanging money, delivering services or goods, working late at night or during the early morning hours, working alone, guarding valuable goods or property and dealing with violent people or volatile situations. The risk factors should not be minimized or misinterpreted. Anyone can become a victim of a workplace assault.

Industries with the greatest risks include:

- The taxi cab industry
- Liquor stores
- Detective/Protective services
- Gas service stations
- Jewelry stores
- Service and retail trade industries
- Nursing homes
- Hospitals
- Restaurants/Bars

Types of Workplace Violence
"Even if you're on the right track, you'll get run over if you just sit there." –Will Rogers

Workplace violence is usually characterized by the following types:

1) EMPLOYER DIRECTED. Described as violence against anyone in workplace authority including, supervisors, managers, directors, department heads, business owners and executives. Employer directed

violence is also the fastest growing type of workplace violence increasing from one homicide per month in 1992 to a current estimate of five or six monthly.

2) DOMESTIC DIRECTED. Generally a partner or would-be partner engages in violence against the object of his or her affection. It has been estimated that domestic violence accounts for $975 million in lost wages for victims in days missed from work. Sexual harassment and everyday domestic disputes have the potential to carry over and invade the workplace and lead to violence.

3) PROPERTY AND COMMERCIALLY DIRECTED. Acts against any property or equipment that the organization owns. It may also include theft of money or property.

The circumstances surrounding workplace violence differ significantly. As a result, different types of awareness must be utilized. This book examines some of the best protection tools an employer can offer to its employees in order to protect them against incidents of workplace violence. Some of the suggestions that will be proposed include the establishment of a Zero Tolerance Workplace Violence Policy, establishing a workplace violence protection program and the incorporation of that information into employee handbooks or manuals that will become standard operating procedures and accident prevention manuals for the organization. Doing nothing is not an acceptable action plan. Something must be done to stop the problem from happening and it must be done now.

CHAPTER TWO

EMPLOYER RESPONSIBILITY & LIABILITY

"Nothing begins and nothing ends, that is not paid with moan; for we are born in other's pain, and perish in our own."

--Francis Thompson

Violence can occur in any aspect of the workplace. While the responsibility to protect and cure is on everyone, realistically the employer is the party who will bear the ultimate responsibility.

It is generally recognized that an employer has a duty to provide a safe workplace for its employees. This requirement is firmly established in the General Duty Clause of the Occupational Safety & Health Act of 1970 (OSHA), (29 USC 651). Under this clause employers have the responsibility to furnish a safe and healthful working environment for employees. The explicit purpose of the Act, as stated by Congress in its findings and declaration of purpose and policy, is to "assure, as far as possible, every working man and woman in the nation safe and healthful working conditions" (29 USC 651(b), 1982). The Act mandates, by its clear and unambiguous language, that in addition to compliance with hazard-specific standards, all employers have a general duty to provide their employees with a workplace free from recognized hazards likely to cause death or serious physical harm.

The OSHA standard and its far reaching requirements are not new, they have existed since the inception of the Act in 1970. The law's purpose is a simple one. It must be used by employers in the development of programs and adherence to guidelines and regulations that will provide a safe and healthful workplace for employees.

In enforcing this mandate, OSHA relies on Section 5(a) of "The General Duty Clause." Employers may be cited for violating this clause if there is a recognized incident (hazard) of workplace violence in their establishment and they do nothing to prevent or abate it. While failure to implement any proposed OSHA guideline may not in itself create a violation of the General Duty Clause, those who act in "good faith" and follow the guidelines are generally not cited for their violation. It is only among the group of employers who choose to do nothing that encounter the wrath of OSHA enforcement.

In addition to the federal law, most states have occupational safety and health statutes which also impose a duty on the employer to provide a safe and healthful working environment for employees. Some of those state standards may place a more stringent requirement on the employer by requiring it to establish, implement and maintain an injury and illness prevention program that will satisfy their statutory obligation to provide a safe working environment with more conviction than the federal law.

As the workplace changes, managing employees with a variety of health-related problems has become an increasingly complex legal challenge. Prior to 1990, state worker's compensation and disability laws determined an employer's duties, obligations and worker benefits. Generally, claims arising out of the employer's breach of this duty (safe workplace) were limited to claims for worker's compensation by employees as their sole and exclusive remedy for such breach. This exclusivity provision remains intact even though the actions of the employer may be characterized as willful, wanton, or intentional.

Under a state worker's compensation statute, a "covered employer" is one with at least one employee and a "covered employee" is an individual incurring an injury that arises out of or in the course of the employment relationship. The exclusivity provisions of the worker's compensation statutes enable an ill or injured worker, or his dependents, legal recovery regardless of fault. They also provide for financial compensation to the worker and ensure the coverage of the costs of medical treatment without the necessity of bringing suit against the employer. These laws also create a protection for employers from negligence suits brought by their employees, a provision commonly referred to as the sole and exclusive remedy aspect of the worker's compensation statute. While workers are generally barred from bringing suit against their employer and must accept worker's compensation payments as their sole remedy if they sustain a work-related illness or injury, they may not be prohibited from seeking legal recourse from third parties. A whole new area of legal liability may be emerging.

Worker's compensation immunity for employers may not extend to intentional torts committed by employers against any of its workers. Exceptions to this rule may include intentional infliction of emotional distress, retaliation and discrimination, sexual assault and workplace violence. Employer's may be held liable for their employee's actions conducted within the scope of their employment under the doctrine of *respondent superior* (let the master answer). To be within the "scope of employment," conduct must meet the following criteria:

1) It must be of the kind the actor was employed to perform;
2) It must occur substantially within the authorized time and space limits; and
3) It must be motivated at least, in part, by a purpose to serve the master.

Under federal and state laws, anti-retaliation provisions have been incorporated into their regulations. These provisions prohibit discrimination or retaliation against employees who elect to exercise their rights under the various safety laws. Penalties for violating these statutes vary, but usually include back pay, reinstatement and other forms of mandatory relief. Also noteworthy is the fact that filing a claim under either the federal or state safety laws will not prevent an employee from suing the employer for wrongful termination or retaliation in violation of public policy. In this area of expanding liability, employers are advised to proceed with caution.

As previously noted, the employer must act to protect its employees against all reasonably foreseeable hazards that arise in the workplace. While a strict liability cause of action may not be available against the employer, employers could find themselves facing a violation of the Act's General Duty Clause because of circumstances related to a work or domestic violence incident that carries over into the workplace, which causes an employee to suffer an on-the-job injury.

In 1992 OSHA issued a standards interpretation and compliance letter on the subject of criminal violence in the workplace, addressing the Act's General Duty Clause, it states:

"(The) Act does require employers to take steps necessary to reduce or eliminate the recognized hazards present which are likely to cause death or serious physical harm to employees . ... it is our legal opinion that an employer could be cited under the General Duty Clause as a result of hazards presented by the potential for criminal acts against its employees in the workplace."

As the above referenced quote suggests, the potential for employer liability can be a natural consequence of workplace violence, therefore, employers must take prompt action to eliminate any form of potential tort liability from occurring. Tort actions such as negligence, negligent hiring, negligent retention and negligent supervision and the failure to warn potential victims of workplace violence could become viable causes of action against an unsuspecting employer. In the latter instance, there is clearly a duty placed upon employers to warn employees of all foreseeable risks of harm, especially in those instances where a specific identifiable threat to an employee has been made in the workplace.

In most cases, and as a necessary part of protecting their legal interests, employers should prepare themselves to deal with the consequences of workplace violence by providing a work environment that promotes and encourages open communication. It is also important that employers develop written procedures for reporting and responding to any type of workplace violence incident. In addition, employers should consider offering and encouraging counseling for their employees whenever a worker is threatened or assaulted in the workplace. Living within the OSHA requirements may, in the long run, be an employer's best and least costly course of action.

The Legal Issues
"To lose is to learn."

--Anonymous

As earlier noted, most state worker's compensation laws provide a remedy for employees who are injured "in the course of employment," however, a new liability trend may be developing. The legal theory currently being tested is that violence in the workplace may constitute an unsafe and dangerous condition for which employers may be liable to an injured employee or third person. Under this theory, a wrongful death action could be developed as an intentional tort exception to the traditional worker's compensation sole and exclusive remedy. The potential for such liability should concern every employer and cause them to take very seriously their legal obligation to make the workplace safe.

In the introductory passage of *The Corporate Counsellor*, March 2000, the following was stated:

"Potential employer liability for workplace violence is well established, and juries tend to be generous with their awards. Most employers believe that state worker's compensation statutes provide the exclusive relief for injuries arising out of an individual's employment. But courts across the country are carving out exceptions to this exclusivity rule by establishing, and rapidly evolving, an intentional tort exception to worker's compensation claims. An intentional tort theory becomes applicable when the nature of an injury does not arise by accident within the employment setting. Employer liability for third-party actions occurs when the employer does not act to prevent or eliminate a known threat. Once the intentional tort exception has been alleged, an injured employee can proceed under a variety of common law theories, including voluntary assumption of a duty to protect, negligent security, negligent failure to warn, negligent hiring, negligent retention, negligent supervision and other potentially expensive torts on which there is no financial cap."

An employer may ask, how does such a duty arise? Quite simply from the employer's express or implied promise under OSHA "to furnish a safe and healthful working environment for employees." For example, when the employer provides security for its workforce, a requirement to provide adequate security is implied. If an employer's security measures are "grossly inadequate," they will likely be forced to pay. As Robert Levin indicated in his legal treatise entitled "Workplace Violence: Navigating Through the Minefield of Legal Liability," the following theories of liability could apply:

NEGLIGENCE. This theory is defined by the Restatement of Torts, §281 as the legal duty to use reasonable care to prevent a foreseeable risk of injury to others, including a breach of that duty. In the workplace, employers have a duty to fulfill OSHA's mandate "to furnish a safe and healthful working environment, to warn employees concerning dangerous conditions, to hire, retain qualified employees, and provide adequate security." An employer's failure to abide by any part of this standard could subject it to a violation of the statute and a subsequent negligence claim.

NEGLIGENT HIRING. This is an independent cause of action that occurs when, prior to the time the employee is actually hired, the employer knew or should have known of the employee's unfitness, and the issue of liability primarily focuses upon the adequacy of the employer's pre-employment investigation into the employee's background. *Garcia* v. *Duffy* 492 S2d 435 (Fla. Dist. Ct. App. 1986). The legal test for a claim of negligent hiring is whether the employer has negligently placed an "unfit" person in an employment situation involving an unreasonable risk of harm to others. *J* v. *Victory Tabernacle Baptist Church,* 236 VA. 206, 372 S.E. 2d 391 (1988). In every instance, the employer has the duty to use reasonable care to investigate an employee's competency and reliability prior to employment. *Pontiacs* v. *K.M.S. Inv.,* 331 N.W. 2d 907, 911 fn.5 (Minn. 1983).

NEGLIGENT RETENTION OR SUPERVISION. This occurs when, during the course of employment, the employer becomes aware or should have become aware of the problem with an employee that indicated his unfitness, and the employer fails to take further action such as investigating, discharge or reassignment. *Garcia* v. *Duffy, supra.* The employer's liability for both causes of action is predicated on the employer's conduct rather than on whether the employee was acting within the course and scope of his/her employment. Negligent retention may also be considered a breach of the employer's duty to be aware of an employee's fitness and to take corrective action through retraining, reassignment, and discharge. The employer must always be careful whenever the job responsibilities of an employee are changed over a period of time (i.e. An employee who is hired to work at a specific site, where he/she is closely supervised and has little contact with others. Later, that employee's job is changed and he/she is free to move to different locations.) At this point, the employer has a duty to conduct further investigation into that employee's past work record.

Clearly the potential for employer liability for injuries that arise in the workplace including those that are attributable to violent acts may extend beyond the worker's compensation statutes. Any deliberate act by the employer with the intent to injure, violations of public policy, discrimination, or willful physical or sexual assaults against another employee, may give rise to liability beyond those noted above. There must be a strong commitment by the employer to provide and maintain a worker-friendly environment that emphasizes safety and health. This will go a long way toward reducing the likelihood of a workplace violence event occurring and in turn may have the added benefit of reducing the employer's risk of legal liability from a third party tort claim should such an incident take place.

CHAPTER THREE

I'LL KNOW IT WHEN I SEE IT -
"RECOGNIZING THE SIGNS"

"Expect trouble as an inevitable part of life and repeat to yourself the most comforting words of all: This, too, shall pass."

--Ann Landers

How do we prepare ourselves to deal with acts of violence in the workplace? This is the million dollar question. While the answers may vary, there is no one answer that will suffice. The best place to start the process is to recognize the warning signs of violence when they begin to emerge.

Workplace violence can happen anywhere, and at any time. No one is immune. Employers and employees alike must become sensitive to the effects of workplace violence and to create a culture that both encourages and promotes open communication within the organization. Usually it is the failure to communicate that becomes the catalyst that begins the chain reaction leading to workplace violence. Fuel is then added to the fire by the employer's failure to properly respond to the situation.

We have learned, and always the hard way, that in almost every incident of workplace violence, before the enraged employee "went off the deep end" and reached their breaking point, they exhibited signs of impending trouble. The most disturbing aspect is the fact that in every case, those signs went undetected, unreported, were ignored or at best, treated lightly, usually resulting in disastrous consequences.

Over and over we have asked ourselves, why the oversight? In dealing with adverse situations, it is easy to turn our back and look the other way, whether the reasons are due to ignorance, fear, indifference or a person's natural desire to avoid confrontation (a trait very common among most people). We must come to the realization that the problem will not go away on its own, no matter how hard we want it to. We must also recognize that confrontation is something most people want to avoid. The thought of having to face someone and tell them something that might result in open hostility, an angry debate or create a potential for violence creates a lot of anxiety. However, procrastination only makes the problem worse. An employee's problem, if ignored and left unaddressed, will soon become everybody's problem, without any forewarning and often with tragic consequences. There are things we can look for and they are set out in the following pages.

The Profile
"Conduct is three-fourths of our life and its largest concern."
--Matthew Arnold

The typical person, the one likely to commit a violent act in the workplace, looks a lot like you and me, except for some very telling outward signs. It is from these signs that the psychologists have developed a profile of a person who is most likely to commit a violent act. While profiling may be viewed by some as stereotyping and therefore inappropriate, the fact remains that many of the exhibited signs developed by the psychologists in the profile highlight individual characteristics that should make us all stop and think.

"Trusting your gut" about the actions of a person who displays these profiled signs may be enough to stop a tragic situation from taking place in your organization. The old adage, "if it doesn't look right, it probably isn't" is likely good advice.

While developing a profile about a person and his/her propensity for violence may be risky, to do nothing is equally problematic. In most cases, the individual who "explodes" into a rage and then becomes violent will likely cause great harm to others. That person will also fit into some aspect of the developed profile.

The profile, which addresses generalities, also identifies common characteristics, such as being antisocial with a sociopathic personality, traits found to be more common in males. That person will also be between 25 - 40 years of age with a history of violence (the most effective criteria for forecasting violent behavior). The person generally is a loner, has a fascination with guns and probably owns several, likes to talk about those guns with others, is an angry person (a prelude to rage that often leads to violence), has no outlet to vent his anger, will usually be withdrawn, has serious personal or family problems (e.g. divorce, death of a close family member, loss of job), is prone to substance or alcohol abuse, frequently displays bizarre behavior, is subject to frequent mood swings and outbursts and is paranoid about others (everyone is out to get him).

The person described in this profile will also have trouble functioning in the workplace. This individual is usually absent or late for work and often requires the attention of management concerning both personal and job related problems, has fluctuating levels of productivity including quality related issues, may be accident prone with a low regard for his own safety and the safety of others, does not get along with co-workers, is often moody and sometimes threatening to others. This person will likely blame others for his failures, disregard personal grooming and health habits (e.g. unkempt hair, dirty clothes) and demonstrates long periods lacking enthusiasm and energy, often displaying signs of persistent depression.

The Signs
"Everyone is a prisoner of his own experiences. No one can eliminate prejudices, just recognize them."
--Edward R. Murrow

The following is a summary of signs taken from cases where workplace violence has occurred. The individuals who committed the acts of violence displayed these signs but they were missed by all who observed them. The exhibited signs and profile bear a close resemblance.

- Severely depressed
- History and fascination with guns
- A desire to cause violence
- Constantly blaming others
- Refusal to accept responsibility for their actions
- Chemical dependency (drugs and/or alcohol)
- Emotionally enraged and often depressed
- Poor performance with decreasing levels of productivity and quality of work
- Prone to mistakes with low levels of concentration
- Strained relationships with their fellow workers
- Aggressive behavior accompanied by a bad/explosive temper

Upon examination of the above criteria, one might conclude that while profiling may be somewhat unpredictable, it certainly can be effective in identifying areas where an employer's concerns should be directed. Remember, the problem is not always with the system but with those who are charged with operating the system.

It is also noteworthy that a person prone to violence and committing violent acts will go through a series of behavioral stages before reaching the "breaking point". Those stages are summarized below:

FIRST STAGE
- Several behavioral changes
- Uncooperative attitude
- Curses profusely
- Constantly argues with co-workers
- Spreads gossip and rumors with intent to harm others
- Makes unwanted sexual comments
- Hostile toward co-workers and customers
- High level of irritability and anxiety
- Appears unrested or tired
- May have trouble sleeping

SECOND STAGE
- Views self as a victim
- Verbalizes a desire to harm others (fellow employees and/or the employer)
- Writes violent or sexual notes
- Steals property or sabotages equipment
- Has a total disregard of company policies and procedures
- Accident prone
- Decreased interest and confidence in their work

THIRD STAGE

- Level of anger intensifies and is often accompanied by emotional outbursts such as fighting, property destruction, use or display of weapons, an expressed desire to harm others, depression and suicidal threats.

How does the profile described earlier fit into the actual cases where workplace violence has occurred? There are usually so many similarities in workplace violence incidents that citing a few examples may tell the complete story. In every incident of workplace violence there were signs that were either missed or ignored. We will first look at some of the missed or ignored signs that were cited in the Lockheed Martin incident which occurred in Meridian, Mississippi in July, 2003.

The following is taken from statements made by co-workers of the Lockheed Martin perpetrator responding to questions from The Associated Press. The sad irony of this incident is that the shooter had undergone anger counseling at least once in the past couple of years and had recently been passed over for a promotion at the plant. Even more alarming is the fact that on the day of the shooting the perpetrator was sitting in a meeting with managers at his factory job, listening to them explain the importance of being honest and responsible in the workplace. At some point during that meeting, this disgruntled employee had heard enough, got up and walked out of the room returning within a few minutes with a shotgun and rifle stating "I told you about (expletive) with me." He sprayed the room with shotgun blasts, killing two. He then proceeded to the factory floor, where the bloody rampage continued and three more workers were killed. When the shooting stopped, five people lay dead and nine more were wounded. The shooter ended the horror by taking his own life.

The husband of one of the victims had this to say about the 48 year-old plant worker who did the shooting. "Obviously, he was a sick guy. I wish somebody had given him some help before he done destroyed my life and my kid's life." Employees from the plant also described the perpetrator as a "hot head" who frequently used racial epithets and made threats against blacks and had a history of run-ins with management and his fellow employees. According to one employee, "(The shooter) was mad at the world. This man had an issue with everybody." "It's just not about race. It was just the excuse he was looking for."

It was also reported by The Associated Press that plant employees had previously expressed concerns to their managers about this individual and counselors were at the plant two years ago to work with him. The shooter even told a union steward, "One of these days, they're going to (expletive) me off and I'm going to come here and shoot some people." Several workers mentioned they were not surprised when (the shooter) was identified. He was described as an individual who talked about wanting to kill people, "I'm capable of doing it," he said.

Another employee said "He threatened me personally" and commented, "I'll come in here and kill all you ... and shoot myself." "It just wasn't one day he told me that. He told me that on several occasions." Sadly, only one of those prior threats were reported to management and that occurred following a comment made in December 2001. However, this worker didn't think (the perpetrator) would carry out the threats. "I'm one of those show-me type persons...Apparently, he was getting ready to show-me."

Now let us compare the comments from the Lockheed Martin incident with the signs mentioned by employees in the Nu-Wood shooting that took place in Goshen, Indiana as summarized in a South Bend Tribune newspaper article entitled "Echoes of Violence, Scars and Memories," written one year after the 2001 incident:

"In statements given to police, co-workers described him (the shooter) as 'nice,' 'mellow,' and 'very friendly.' The 36-year old enjoyed guns and hunting, friends said, they knew he was a licensed gun dealer, but no one thought of him as violent. He liked to talk about guns and how he liked to shoot ... But I never expected him to do anything like (he did) ... I don't know what was going through the guy's mind. Some people thought it could have been love, the unrequited kind. (The shooter) was smitten with a woman who worked at the plant. It's unclear how she felt about him ... but (he) felt she was having a relationship with a third plant employee. She wanted to break up with him and that stressed him out."

It was also noted by other witnesses that the NuWood perpetrator "hadn't slept in days ... and was acting strange that Thursday morning." It was reported that "he challenged the other men to a fight. He talked 'nonsense' about having his pants pulled down, people said." "So the plant manager talked to him (he was told he wasn't fired), sent him home for the day and offered to help him get treatment. He agreed, they said, and headed home to get some sleep." "Two and half hours after he left Nu-Wood, (he) drove back in his red pick-up, came in the front door, and started shooting." "An autopsy showed he had no drugs or medication in his system when he died ... no one will ever know exactly what drove (him) to come back with his 12-gauge shotgun ... (the reason) died with Bobby", said his mother.

Very sad and tragic statements but so common in almost every workplace violence incident. It is important that both employers and employees alike become proactive when these signs arise in the workplace. Recognizing and providing help to employees living under unusual stresses in their daily lives may be as important as providing medical care.

The burden rests squarely on the shoulders of the employer to recognize and understand the warning signs in order to prevent a tragedy before it happens. This is not an easy task. Unfortunately, we have failed in this regard. Despite the past failures, employers must remain on high alert to recognize the early warning signs and to do everything in their power to prevent an incident from happening. Simply ignoring the problem will not make it go away. Employers and employees alike must learn to trust their instincts. They must pay attention to their "gut feeling" that something might be wrong and of course, trust that feeling. If you believe that a co-worker is dangerous or might be dangerous, you must act on it before the danger level increases. Learning to trust your judgment and instincts is critical. When you get that feeling, learn to go with it. While nothing can guarantee that an incident of workplace violence will not occur, communication and awareness in any workplace violence prevention program is usually the first step in reducing the likelihood of such an occurrence.

Remember, in every case of workplace violence there are early warning signs. Employers and employees must learn to recognize those signs and act on them. When you look you must see, when you listen you must hear. Equally as important, you must trust your gut. If something looks wrong, it probably is. If you think someone is or may be dangerous, treat the situation as if it is dangerous. Discipline yourself to not ignore the signs.

CHAPTER FOUR

STRESS

"Nothing is more destined to create deep-seated anxiety in people than the false assumption that life should be free from anxieties."
--Archbishop Fulton J. Sheen

For most people stress is considered a normal part of life, so they just try to deal with it. There seems to be an acceptance of the idea that the world is racing ahead so you better hurry up or you will get left behind. This is dangerous thinking. Many experts agree that a regular dose of stress on the human body is a contributory cause of serious health problems such as cancer, heart attack, stroke, high blood pressure and gastrointestinal diseases.

As the nature of the workplace changes, so does the level of stress we experience as part of our everyday normal life. High levels of stress, which are an unsettling condition caused by a variety of adverse external influences, pose a threat to the health of everyone, individuals as well as organizations. Stress often leads to anger, then rage, and the likelihood of an act of violence in the workplace taking place is enhanced.

Bill D. Hager, in an article entitled "Simple 'Stress Busters' Relieve Burnout and Worker's Compensation Costs" made the following observations:

All over America, employees are working harder than ever. Professionals labor an average of almost 44 hours a week. In some fields, such as law, medicine or finance, employees are often expected to work twice that much. U.S. factory employees work 430 more hours annually – the equivalent of 2½ months more – than their peers in Germany.

With every extra hour and new demand, the price employees and the companies they work for pay in stress keeps mounting. Among the eye-opening trends that emerged from interviews with a cross-section of about 600 American workers: One in three Americans seriously thought about quitting work because of job stress, and one in three expects to "burn out" on the job in the near future. One in three say job stress is the single greatest stress in their life.

Significant burnout occurred among workers whose companies had substantially cut employee benefits, changed ownership, required frequent overtime, or reduced the workforce. Seven in ten workers say job stress lowers their productivity, and they experience frequent health ailments.

No doubt about it – workplace stress is a full-fledged epidemic in the '90s. Unfortunately, so is relentless, stress-inducing workplace change. Pick up the paper on any given day and read all about it: organizations across a broad range of industries scaling down staff and budget, restructuring and reengineering operations, reinventing their corporate culture, changing management teams, or changing ownership.

All social, business and economic indicators point to more of the same for the foreseeable future. In the meantime, the high price of unattended job stress leaves no one unscathed. Workers fight an assortment of physical and psychological ailments, including exhaustion, anger, anxiety, headaches and insomnia. Employers are confronted with higher turnover, lower productivity, more frequent absenteeism and greater health care costs.

Stress can become a violence factor. On the one hand, a violent situation in the home or the workplace will likely lead to stress. On the other hand, stress may also be the catalyst that causes violence at home or in the workplace because it surfaces in an individual in a variety of different ways. The accelerated pace of our lives, technological changes, domestic problems and the increase of drug and alcohol use and abuse are just a few examples of what have become our everyday stressors. No one is immune because stress has become a regular part of our daily lives and it effects all of us. It has an affect on our family lives and our jobs. It has become a rather common but serious problem in the American workplace.

Stress Defined
"Life is just one damned thing after another."
                                        --Frank Ward O'Malley

"Stress has become a buzzword; it seems to explain everything, yet explain nothing ... we use it in place of other words is the problem. Words like 'I'm angry', 'I feel frightened', 'I'm exhausted' and 'I'm sad' ... we say 'I'm stressed out' instead of 'I need to cry' ... if we don't stop to realize what we are feeling ... if we lump all our emotion under the word 'stress' ... it is hard for us to figure out what we need in order to feel better ... 'stress' is not a feeling, it is the RESULT of stifled feelings and needs. It is a symptom, not a diagnosis." Scott N., "Stress Has Become the New Buzzword," South Bend Tribune (August 27, 1988).

Stress can be defined as the kind of pressure that strains or upsets a balanced system. Webster's New World™ College Dictionary defines stress as a "strain or straining force ... a force extended upon a body ... mental or emotional tension or strain characterized by feelings of anxiety, fear, etc. ... a combination of factors that causes such tension or strain, as an urgent need or perceived threat." In psychological terms, stress is defined as "a condition typically characterized by symptoms of mental and physical tension or strain, as depression or hypertension, that can result from a reaction to a situation in which a person feels threatened, pressured, etc." On the job stress is defined as "the harmful physical and emotional responses that occur when the requirements of the job do not match the capabilities, resources, or needs of the worker."

When the challenges of the workplace cannot be met, anxiety and pressure increase. Relaxation turns to exhaustion and satisfaction turns to stress. When stressful situations go unresolved, the body's nervous system is kept in a constant state of activation, which can wear down the biological system. When this occurs, a person's life is now set for a number of negative reactions such as the potential for illness, injury, and job failure. An individual's shortcomings, whether job-related or personal, are often viewed as failures and this frustration may become a source of personal rage. Rage is nothing more than an intense form of anger and if left unchecked, it will grow and develop over time, eventually leading to violence.

Causes of Job Stress

"Achievement is largely the product of steadily raising one's level of aspiration and expectation."

— *Jack Nicklaus*

The theories of Sigmund Freud, who defined the sources of happiness and contentment in life as the need for love and the need to work, and Abraham Maslow, who established the "Hierarchy of Human Needs," both set out in their own terms one common fact: work is an important part of a person's life. Society looks at the workplace as a source of friendships, order and structure in a person's life, providing routine, stability and a sense of purpose. When this important aspect of a person's life is disrupted (a change in position, income, or opportunity), stress, rage and violence in the form of retaliating action, is the likely result.

Maintaining proper employee health means allowing them to have some element of control over their workflow and rewarding them for their contributions to the organization. Employees who feel they are being treated fairly at work are less likely to develop health-related disabilities such as cardiovascular problems, back pain and fewer workplace injuries.

Differences in a person's individual characteristics, such as personality and coping style, will dictate whether changes in job conditions will affect them positively or negatively. What may be stressful for one person may not be stressful to another. Regardless of how it affects us, stress is a problem for both employers and employees alike, as evidenced by this reference to the 1995 Worker's Compensation Yearbook which noted that "by 1995, nearly one-half of the states allowed worker's compensation claims for emotional disorders and disability are due to stress on the job." The passage of time has not diminished the problem but it has provided employers with both the means and methods for dealing with the problem.

How To Approach Job Stress - Making Lemonade out of Lemons
"Speak when you are angry and you will make the best speech you will ever regret."
--Ambrose Bierce

There is little doubt that working conditions play an important part in the creation of job stress. While specific factors in a person's personality certainly enter into the equation, an individual's exposure to stressful working conditions can and usually does have a direct effect on his/her personal safety and health.

There may be factors in an individual's life that could help reduce the effects of stress at work, such as a balance between family or personal life and work, a support network of friends and co-workers and a relaxed and positive outlook. However, these factors are often over- shadowed by adverse conditions that arise in the job setting which can lead to stress. Let us take a look at a few of those factors as cited by the U.S. Department of Health and Human Services Center for Disease Control and Prevention.

Design of Tasks: Heavy workload, infrequent rest breaks, long work hours and shift work; as well as hectic and routine tasks that have little inherent meaning, do not utilize a workers' skill, and provide little sense of control (i.e. working to a point of exhaustion, allowing little room for flexibility or rest).

Management Style: Lack of participation by workers in the decision-making process, poor communication in the organization and the lack of family-friendly policies may also be contributors (i.e. a company needs to be sensitive to individual or family needs).

Interpersonal Relationships: A poor social environment that lacks support or help from co-workers and supervisors (i.e. job isolation that diminishes the chance to interact with other employees) may contribute to stress.

Work Roles: Conflicting, uncertain or unreasonable job expectations, having too much responsibility, or too many "hats to wear" (i.e. employee is caught in the dilemma of trying to please everybody including meeting company needs and customer expectations), may also contribute to stress.

Career Concerns: There is a feeling of job insecurity, opportunity for growth, advancement, or promotion. There are many changes taking place for which the workers are unprepared (i.e. numerous changes in the workplace, a growing concern about their future).

Environmental Conditions: Unpleasant or dangerous physical conditions such as crowding, noise, air pollution or ergonomically unfriendly work.

How Does Stress Affect our Health?
To rule one's anger is well; to prevent it is still better."

--Tyron Edwards

Stress is the factor that puts the brain in gear. It sets off an internal alarm whereby the brain tells the body that something is happening. The body's response to stress is to prepare for defensive action. In more exact terms, when stress occurs, the nervous system is alerted and hormones are released throughout the body to sharpen senses. The pulse quickens, respiration increases and the muscles become tense. This reaction, sometimes referred to as the "fight or flight" response, helps the body prepare itself to defend against the impending threat, whether that threat is real or perceived. While everyone's human system responds in the same way, as individuals we all handle it differently.

The short-lived or infrequent stress episode will cause little risk to the body. However, left unchecked or unresolved, the body will remain in a constant "fight" state, causing greater wear and tear to occur. The result is usually fatigue and a lessening of the body's ability to quickly respond and defend itself against further harm. The risk of injury, illness or disease is thereby enhanced.

The Brain, Anxiety and Fear
"The only thing we have to fear is fear itself."

--Franklin D. Roosevelt

To get at the essence of anxiety, one must start with the anatomy of fear. As earlier noted, the focal point of all this activity is the brain, which is designed to promote survival of the individual in his environment.

"An activated amygdala* doesn't wait around for instructions from the conscious mind. Once it perceives a threat, it can trigger a body wide emergency response within milliseconds." (G. Cowley, "Our Bodies, Our Fears," Newsweek, February, 2003).

*The amygdala is a small round mass of gray matter in the front part of the temporal lobe of the brain.

To better understand the effects of anxiety and stress on the body, we must examine the so called "fear factor." The brain is programmed to promote survival of the human being in the environment. Survival in this instance "depends on the ability of the organism to respond to threat or reward, and predict the circumstances under which they are likely to occur."

When the brain perceives a threat, it will trigger an alert notice in the form of a body-wide emergency response. This notice will cause the stress hormones to divert the body's resources to either fighting or fleeing. When this occurs, the heart will pound and the muscles begin to pump, receiving an energizing blast of glucose. The stress hormones then begin to act on the brain, creating an internal state of high alert. At the same time, the circuitry involved in memory formation will become supercharged. During this process, the stress hormones usually divert the body's resources from other critical areas and extensive collateral damage may result. The release of these stress hormones into the body is likely to create a dangerous situation.

During any stressful situation, the brain will react by signaling the body and placing it on alert status. When this happens, the following chain reaction takes place in the person's body:

- the heart beats faster
- breathing quickens so that more oxygen can be taken in
- blood pressure rises
- the liver releases sugar into the blood stream, increasing energy
- the person begins to sweat (the perspiration increase is intended to regulate body temperature)
- the stomach vessels constrict to force blood to other parts of the body
- the arms and legs become beneficiaries of extra blood for energy
- the body is now poised for "fight or flight"

The accumulation of stress, especially when it occurs in frequent situations, can have a long term effect on the body. The body's constant responses to stressful situations keeps the "fight or flight" reaction in high gear. This high state of alertness will simply wear the body down. Some common symptoms associated with high stress levels are impaired memory, high blood pressure, a weakening of the immune system and stomach ulcers. Chronic anxiety or stress will in the long run take its toll and its long term effect on the human body can be very serious. To have relief, the affected individual must maintain an element of control at all times and learn to deal with his concerns in a natural manner, always in a position to adapt to the world that he must live and work in. Easier said than done.

The Journal of Occupational and Environmental Medicine has reported that health care expenditures were nearly 50% greater for workers who reported high levels of stress. Why should this be a concern for employers? Primarily because as a result of continuous stress a list of common problems has developed. They include headaches, difficulty in concentration, short temper, mood swings and sleep disturbances, upset stomach, job dissatisfaction, low morale and disturbed relationships with family and friends.

While the early signs of stress may be easily recognizable, the long term effects of job stress on the more chronic diseases that could affect a person's health are more difficult to diagnose. These generally take longer to develop. The Encyclopedia of Occupational Safety and Health noted that the following diseases and injuries can be attributed to stress based upon its research studies.

Cardiovascular Disease: Many studies suggest that psychologically demanding jobs that allow employees little control over the work process increase the risk of cardiovascular disease.

Musculoskeletal Disorders: On the basis of research by NIOSH and many other similar organizations, it is widely believed that job stress increases the risk for the development of back and upper-extremity musculoskeletal disorders.

Psychological Disorders: Several studies suggest that differences in rates of mental health problems (such as depression and burnout) for various occupations are due partly to differences in job stress levels. (Economic and lifestyle differences between occupations may also be a contributing factor.)

Workplace Injury: There is a growing concern that stressful working conditions may interfere with safe work practices thereby setting the stage for the likelihood of an increase in job related injuries occurring at work.

Suicide, Cancer, Ulcers and Impaired Immune Function: Some studies also suggest that there may be a relationship between stressful working conditions and these health problems. However, research in this area is far from being conclusive.

It is important that in every stressful situation the employer and the employee learn to maintain control and recognize how to deal with their concerns as a natural response to the environment in which they are required to work. In doing so they will be better able to handle the physical (and mental) challenges that stress creates.

How Can We Prevent Job Stress?
"The healthy, the strong individual, is the one who asks for help when he needs it. Whether he has an abscess on his knee or in his soul."

--Rona Barrett

Some of the first signs of job stress are low morale, job complaints, increased absenteeism and high turnover; there may be no clues other than decreasing efficiency and productivity. Whatever signs might exist, the concerned employer must take immediate notice and then act promptly. Taking the following steps is important:

Identify the Problem: Involve your employees to help identify the source of the problem. Discussions among management, labor representatives (if there is a union on site) and employees are not only a great place to start but it may prove to be a valuable resource. The employer must be industrious when gathering information about employee perceptions and opinions relating to their jobs, including their perceived levels of stress and job satisfaction. The employer must then summarize the information learned and analyze it fully in order to pinpoint the source of the employee dissatisfaction (stress).

Design and Implement: Once the sources of work stress have been identified and the problem understood, the employer is now in a better position to design and implement a strategy to reduce stress or prevent its reoccurrance. It may be necessary for the employer to improve communications, add stress management training or redesign certain aspects of its business operation. Whatever the intervention strategy, the employer must be sure to communicate the action plan to the employees and tell them when they can expect it to happen.

Evaluate the Interventions: This is an important step in the stress reduction process because it is an opportunity for the employer to determine whether the changes it has implemented are producing the desired result. The employer should consider developing short and long term evaluation periods, quarterly or annually, and stick with them. The employer must focus on the same types of information, such as employee working conditions, levels of perceived stress, health problems and job satisfaction. It may also be wise to include objective criteria such as absenteeism and health care costs as a measurement tool in order to find out if what is being done is working.

More About Preventing Job Stress
"The chief cause of stress is reality."

--Lily Tomlin

Unfortunately, there is no simple "how to" manual or standardized approach for dealing with stress in the workplace, nor have any programs been designed to prevent it. Employers often assume that stress in the workplace is a natural consequence of the setting, that is, work equals stress. By turning up the pressure of work on employees, most employers believe that increased productivity and profitability will result. However, the studies done in this area dispute this conclusion. In fact they indicate just the opposite.

In reality, stressful working conditions are usually associated with increases in tardiness, absenteeism, high turnover, job dissatisfaction and employee burnout. These residual effects of stress have a negative impact on the workplace and, more importantly, the employer's bottom line. A healthy organization is an efficient and productive organization. Low stress levels often equate to higher levels of productivity. This makes finding the cure a priority for the employer and a challenging task. The following ideas are suggested as a starting point:

- Introduce respect and dignity into the work setting.
- Make it a common practice to recognize employees for good work performance.
- Develop an internal value system that promotes honesty and integrity.
- Plan and develop management actions that are consistent with achieving the highest organizational values.

To be a successful enterprise, actions to reduce job stress must be given a top priority, even above those that are related to improving working conditions. In addition, stress management training combined with an Employee Assistance Program can be beneficial to employees by helping them cope with the stress caused by difficult work situations. A well-organized and properly conducted stress management program may also have the added advantage of being easy to implement and possibly less expensive. In order for such programs to be effective they must be focused on the worker and not his or her environment.

By identifying the stressful aspects of the workplace and taking steps to reduce or eliminate their effect on the employee, employers will be able to create a work environment that is effective, efficient, productive, and profitable.

When Do We Start?
"Life is not the way it's supposed to be. It's the way it is. The way we cope with it is what makes the difference."
                                                        --Virginia Satin

The when is NOW! A delayed response to dealing with a stressful work environment will only compound the problem. As earlier noted, the first step toward reducing stress is to create positive change. Employers must act to identify the problems, evaluate them and begin the process of taking steps to remedy them. The wise employer will do the following:

- Ensure that an employee's workload is in line with his or her individual capabilities.
- Design jobs that provide meaning, stimulation and opportunities that fully utilize the employees' skills.
- Define the worker's role and responsibilities in the work setting.

- Allow employees an opportunity to participate in the decision-making process as it relates to their jobs.
- Reduce job uncertainty by improving communications about career enhancement and future employment opportunities within the organization.
- Encourage opportunities for social interaction among workers.
- Establish work schedules that are compatible with the demands and responsibilities both within the job and outside the job.

(American Psychologist, 1990)

In a research study conducted by Northwestern National Life, the following ten employer actions were found to be especially effective in reducing the onset and development of stress-related conditions in employees.   Most of these suggestions cost little or nothing to initiate.

- Allow employees to talk freely with one another. Employees thrive in an atmosphere where they can consult colleagues about work issues and learn to defuse stress with humor.
- Reduce personal conflicts on the job. Treating employ-ees fairly and defining job expectations clearly are two significant steps companies can take to minimize conflicts.
- Give employees adequate control of how they do their work. Managers who are not afraid to let employees make decisions – and learn from their mistakes – foster an atmosphere that reduces stress and increases job satisfaction.
- Ensure that staffing and expense budgets are adequate. Employees overburdened by heavy workloads, high

expectations and inadequate budgets frequently suffer high stress levels.

- Talk openly with employees. Management should keep employees informed about bad news as well as good news. Giving employees opportunities to air their concerns to management is also important.
- Support employee efforts. Workers are better able to cope with heavy workloads if management is sympathetic, understanding and encouraging.
- Provide competitive vacation benefits. Workers who have time to relax and recharge after working hard are less likely to develop stress-related illnesses.
- Maintain current levels of employee benefits. As benefits go down, stress levels go up. Employers must carefully weigh the savings gained from benefit reductions with the potentially high costs associated with employee burnout.
- Reduce the amount of red tape for employees. Employers can lower burnout rates if they ensure that an employees' time is not wasted on unnecessary paperwork and procedures.
- Recognize and reward employees for their accomplishments and contributions. A pat on the back, a public word of praise, a raise, or a bonus can pay employers big dividends in higher employee morale and productivity.

Remember, job stress and its prevention does not end with the implementation of any of the above noted programs. The employer must become proactive in its program development and employees and managers must work together in learning about stress and its effect on the workplace. Only then will positive results begin to emerge.

Recognizing and staying in touch with the signs of stress in the workplace combined with the establishment of a well defined counseling and assessment program (Employee Assistance Program), is just plain smart management. Employers should coach, support, direct and encourage the resolution of work-related problems and they must posture themselves in a position where they can positively influence the employee's work environment on a daily basis. If left unchecked or improperly monitored, a buildup of life and work stresses can overwhelm the employee leading them to a breaking point. When this occurs, stress will likely turn to rage and rage will turn into violence with usually disastrous consequences. The well managed organization, one that stays in touch with the daily issues associated with workplace stress, will find itself in a better position to act when the stress levels reach their highest point.

Understanding the signs, recognizing them when they occur and acting on them in a timely manner are critical steps in the early detection and prevention process. Controlling stress in the workplace is an important first step in reducing the likelihood of violence occurring in your organization.

CHAPTER FIVE

DEVELOPING A WORKPLACE VIOLENCE
PREVENTION PROGRAM AND POLICY

*"The only limit of our realization of tomorrow will be
our doubts of today. Let us move forward with strong
and active faith."*

-- Franklin D. Roosevelt

Before we can attack the problem of workplace violence,
we must understand it. We can only understand it if we
create a system that provides for documenting all violent
incidents that occur in the workplace. (Similar to the OSHA
requirement for reporting workplace injuries and illnesses.)

OSHA Reporting
"All the strength you need to achieve anything is within you."
--Sara Henderson

We spoke earlier of OSHA's General Duty Clause. As
mandated by that Act, employers are also required to annually
report workplace incidents, including those involving
violence, that result in:

1) the hospitalization of three or more employees, or
2) a fatality.
(OSHA, 29 CFR Section 1904.8)

All oral reports that meet the above requirements must be made within eight hours to the nearest OSHA office or appropriate state OSHA enforcement agency.

OSHA also requires that employers maintain a log and summary of all recordable occupational injuries and illnesses sustained by employees in the employers workplace, 29 CFR Section 1904.2. An injury or illness is recordable if it is "work-related" and meets one of the general recording criteria. An injury or illness is also "work-related" if it either caused or contributed to the resulting condition or "significantly" aggravated a pre-existing injury or illness.

All of the above information must be recorded on OSHA's Form 300: "Log of Work-Related Injuries and Illnesses." Employers are also required to complete an injury and illness incident report (OSHA Form 301) or an equivalent form for each injury or illness that is recorded on Form 300. This information must be entered on the form by the employer, within seven calendar days of receiving information that a recordable injury or incident has occurred.

Employers are required to then use this recorded information to create an annual summary of injuries and illnesses and to post that summary in their business no later than February 1 of each year. The annual summary, and the OSHA 301 Incident Report forms, must then be saved by the employer for five years following the end of the year that the records cover. Employers are also obligated, during the records storage period, to update the OSHA 300 logs by reporting any changes that have occurred in the classification of previously recorded injuries and illnesses.

Another important aspect of this reporting process is the requirement that all injuries and illnesses that occur as a result of workplace violence are also recorded when the event occurs on the employer's premises. If the event occurs off the employer's premises, it must be recorded if the worker has engaged in work related activities, or was present at the site of the event as a condition of employment.

The timely and accurate recording of information regarding work-related injuries and illness is essential for later assessing the nature and magnitude of any given incident that occurs in the employer's workplace and for establishing its risk. This information can later be used to assess whether the need for action exists and whether an intervention strategy will be necessary to reduce or mitigate that risk. The intervention strategy may be something that is identifiable to a particular industry or something new and unique as a means for assessing risks of workplace violence. Whatever strategy is used by the employer, like the workplace prevention policy, it must be publicized throughout the organization. As information is acquired, an employer's strategies should be adjusted to fit the circumstances of the situation.

Developing A Written Policy of Zero Tolerance
"The greatest of faults, I should say, is to be conscious of none."

--Carlyle

Any employer policy on workplace violence should provide a strategic approach to dealing with the problem. The employer's policy, aside from having the obvious requirement of thoroughness, must be written in readable terms, designed to deliver a clear but simple message to everyone: managers, staff and all other affected parties. The policy must also demonstrate the employer's commitment and endorsement from every level of the organization, from the top down. This endorsement is a top priority to the success of any violence prevention program. Simply stated, an employer's priority should be to develop a policy, have it endorsed by top management and promote the commitment to *zero tolerance of violence at work* throughout the organization.

Every organization should have an internal reporting mechanism for dealing with workplace violence similar to the policy that deals with sexual harassment or any other form of prohibited discriminatory conduct. If your company, school, college or work setting does not have a policy or plan for dealing with violence, you need to begin drafting one now.

When developing such policies, be sure to create those that prohibit every type of violent behavior such as fighting, making threats, possession of weapons, coercion, use or possession of alcohol, drugs and other controlled substances, disorderly conduct of any type, including fighting or using obscene, abusive or threatening language, defacing or damaging company property and any other conduct likely to harm, injure or kill employees or cause property damage.

There is also a need to include in this policy, threat assessment teams to which violent incidents can be reported. In developing such teams, employers should consider including representatives from human resources, employees and unions (if applicable), security personnel, members of management, employee assistance programs, local law enforcement, and legal department personnel.

Employers are urged to develop programs or plans that would allow them to accurately assess all threats of violence (i.e. how specific is the threat, does the person making the threat have the means for carrying it out), and what steps can be taken to prevent the threat from being carried out.

When a threat of violence occurs among co-workers, firing the perpetrator may or may not be the most effective way of reducing the risk for future violence. As an employer, you may want to retain some control over the individual and require or provide counseling. The employer's violence prevention policy should therefore explicitly state the consequences of making threats or committing acts of violence in the workplace.

Any comprehensive workplace violence prevention policy and program should also include procedures and responsibilities to be taken in the event of a violent incident in the workplace. How is the response team assembled? Who is responsible for taking care of the victims? How will stress debriefing be handled? Who will deal with the families of victims and co-workers? Have Employee Assistance Programs (EAP) been developed? How will the EAP be implemented? Have local mental health and emergency service personnel been alerted or available for assistance? Every employer must know and have the answers to these questions well in advance of a violent situation occurring in the workplace. You know what they say about an ounce of prevention...

(Refer to the Appendix Section for sample policies)

CHAPTER SIX

TAKING STEPS TO PREVENT WORKPLACE VIOLENCE

"The optimist proclaims that we live in the best of all worlds and the pessimist fears this is true."
-- Branch Cabell

As previously noted, it is virtually impossible for any employer to guarantee that its workplace will be free from violence. That just is not going to happen. However, there are many things an employer can and should do to prevent or at least minimize the likelihood of an incident of workplace violence occurring in its organization.

We already addressed the importance of having a written policy that emphasizes Zero Tolerance and the development of a violence control plan that creates an action and reaction team to deal with any incident of workplace violence. Here are some other steps that an employer can take to reduce the likelihood of a workplace violence event occurring.

- *Hire the best candidates:* In fulfilling this requirement, the employer must be sure to know the applicant's job skills and qualifications as well as his/her fitness to perform the job. A well planned and thorough pre-employment process that details an applicant's background, beside helping the employer find the "best" applicant, may also prove to be a valid defense to a claim of negligent hiring in the event of a situation gone bad.

- *Carefully screen all applicants for employment:* This includes conducting in-depth interviews and the signing of releases that authorize the employer to conduct background and reference checks. Train those who have the responsibility for hiring to recognize behavioral and psychological patterns that may need to be explored. This may include investigating all time gaps in a person's work history and verifying all of the applicant's licenses and credentials. Degrees and dates of all previous employment should also be verified before offering the candidate a position. Employers may also want to eliminate applicants who display a temperamental attitude, like those who openly "bad mouth" their last employer.

- *Consider testing job applicants:* While this can quickly become an expensive undertaking with possible legal entanglements, it is nonetheless something for the employer to consider. Tests may include psychological, drug and alcohol, honesty tests and post- offer medical examinations. There are many prohibitions that exist against asking questions related to an applicant's disability (physical, mental, actual or perceived), arrest records, race, pregnancy, marital status, credit history, medical history and prior worker compensation claims. The applicant's rights under the law, including the right to privacy, have a high priority. More importantly, the employer is responsible for knowing its legal obligations under all of the various employment laws, both federal and state. When conducting the hiring process, employers are advised to consult with qualified legal counsel before taking on this aspect of the employment process. Proceed with caution in this area.

- *Provide on-going training and instruction to all employees:* When training your management and supervisory staff, the wise employer will provide information that will help them recognize the early warning signs of potentially violent behavior. Training topics for consideration should include: Discriminatory and Harassment Prevention; Sexual Harassment Prevention; Workplace Violence Prevention; E-Mail and Internet Use; Interviewing and Hiring Skills and Techniques; Substance Abuse Prevention; and Proper Management Techniques for Disability Leaves. Employers are also urged to consider supplemental topics on conflict resolution, handling stress and preparing for the administration of discipline and terminations (topics which are addressed in this book).

- *Provide adequate workplace security.* This may include the development of emergency signaling, alarms and monitoring systems and possibly metal detectors; also installing security cameras and good lighting in parking lots and hallways and providing security escorts to parking lots at night. Access to and from the workplace must also be controlled. The number of entries and exits should be limited and doors should be locked from the outside to prevent easy access to the building. *Do not lock the doors on the inside.* This can create a safety hazard with serious legal consequences should an internal emergency, such as a fire, occur.

- *Develop a warning system:* This is necessary when a threat of a violence is imminent. There may also be a legal duty placed on the employer to warn employees of any direct threats of violence made against an employee. The failure of the employer to act in any crisis situation may result in a violation of its obligation to provide a "safe and healthful" workplace. In any instance of internal crisis, members of management should always make themselves readily accessible to employees.

• *Make available an Employee Assistance Program that includes counseling:* An independent, professional and confidential counseling service should be a part of every employer's workplace violence program. The service can be voluntary or mandatory and made easily accessible for employees.

An Employee Assistance Program or EAP, as it is commonly referred, is nothing more than a program supported by management, designed to offer professional and confidential counseling, usually by an independent outside treatment group, to employees who are troubled. This trouble may result from problems encountered in the workplace or outside of it (e.g. drug and alcohol abuse, health conditions, domestic problems or other personal issues.)

The EAP should be open to employees and their families and designed to assist the employee and his/her family members through the processing of referrals to outside counseling. Employees may enter the program voluntarily or through manager or supervisor referral. The programs should be confidential and their costs are often covered by the sponsoring organization, its insurance plan or a combination of the two. EAPs can be an effective alternative when direct intervention by the employer has not succeeded or professional expertise beyond that normally found within an organization is required.

While an EAP may not be an instant solution or cure for an employee's performance problems, they nonetheless have been proven effective in preventing and improving an employee's medical and emotional well being. With a little effort EAP programs can be designed to help everyone - the employee, his family and the organization. By assessing problems and referring clients to the appropriate assistance, EAP's help employees overcome the personal problems that can affect both health and job performance - issues including family or marital problems, finances, legal difficulties or drug/alcohol abuse. The EAP is a support method that allows an organization to help itself by helping its employees restore themselves to a more normal and productive work life.

- *Other considerations for the employer:*

  - Modifying cash-handling policies such as using locked drop boxes and posting signs and notices that speak to the limited availability of cash.
  - Physically separating workers from customers, clients or the general public through the use of physical barriers, including those that are bullet proof.
  - Have adequate insurance coverage in place to protect against the losses that could result from an incident of workplace violence.
  - Ready access to courts and the possible use of restraining orders and injunctions.

In a workplace violence event, or in any situation where an immediate threat of violence exists, all of an organization's internal resources (legal, human resources, management personnel) and external resources (employee assistance providers, community mental health and law enforcement) should be utilized in order to create a quick and effective response. Minimizing the risk of injury, suffering and loss of life must be every organization's number one priority. Employers should also remember to always document their efforts with regard to every action and prevention step it undertakes in a workplace violence situation. The price for not doing it may be prohibitive.

Summary of Things an Employer Can Do to Diffuse a Workplace Violence Situation

"Life is an unanswered question, but let's still believe in the dignity and importance of the question."

--Tennessee Williams

1) Respond promptly to all reported threats of violence or weapons in the workplace.

2) Promptly and thoroughly investigate all reports of harassment and complaints of abusive conduct.

3) Seek advice and communicate with other people in the organization whenever unusual circumstances arise.

4) Maintain confidentiality when investigating workplace violence complaints and be sure to conduct investigations and counseling sessions privately and discreetly.

5) Take prompt action to suppress defamatory or inflammatory rumors.

6)   Develop a clear policy that prohibits harassment in the workplace and always take prompt action to remedy any form of harassment.
7)   Following the filing of a complaint and investigation of harassment, always let the complaining party know the action taken and the results.
8)   Encourage employees to use the internal complaint procedure developed by the employer to deal with any form of harassment or violent activity in the workplace.
9)   Promptly remove employees impaired by the use of alcohol, drugs and other controlled substances in the workplace or on company owned property.
10)   Screen all job applicants and thoroughly investigate their backgrounds and credentials.

Do's and Don'ts That May Help Diffuse a Volatile Workplace Situation
Compassion for yourself translates into compassion for others."

-- Suku Jay Munsell

Following these simple rules may help you avoid or eliminate an incident of workplace violence.

DO'S:

• DO present a calm and caring attitude and move and speak slowly, quietly and confidentially.
• DO focus your attention on the other person to let them know you are interested in what they have to say.

- DO maintain a relaxed but attentive posture and always position yourself at a right angle from the other person, not directly in front of them.
- DO accept criticism in a positive way. If the complaint is true, say "You are probably right" or "It was my fault." If the criticism is unwarranted, ask questions to clarify the situation.
- DO acknowledge the person's feelings ("I know you are frustrated"). Let them know you understand that they are upset.
- DO evaluate each workplace situation for potential violence when you enter an area and begin the process of relating to the worker.
- DO learn to become vigilant throughout the encounter with the other person.
- DO keep an open path for exiting the area. Avoid letting the potentially violent person stand between you and the door.
- DO call for assistance when necessary.
- DO report any violent incidents to your management.

MORE DO'S FOR THE WORKPLACE:

- Treat others with respect.
- Get to know the people around you.
- Look for ways to improve communication in your office, department or organization.
- Look for ways to improve working conditions.
- Learn to work safely.
- Look for the warning signs of violence.
- Encourage others to be alert for the danger signs in co-workers.
- Listen for verbal abuse on the job.

- Be aware of behavioral changes in your fellow workers.
- Attend safety and training programs to learn how to recognize, avoid or diffuse potentially violent situations.

DON'TS:

- DON'T reject all of the person's demands from the start.
- DON'T become aggressive in your behavior or use a style of communication that generates hostility (i.e. moving rapidly, getting too close, touching, coldness or apathy).
- DON'T make sudden or threatening movements. Control the tone, volume and rate of your speech.
- DON'T challenge, threaten or dare the person. Never belittle, demean or make the person feel foolish.
- DON'T minimize the seriousness of the situation.
- DON'T invade the individual's personal space. Try to keep a distance of 3' to 6' between you and the other person.
- DON'T isolate yourself with a potentially violent person. Let someone else know who you will be meeting with, and where.

CHAPTER SEVEN

LEARNING TO STAY CALM WHEN
DEALING WITH WORKPLACE VIOLENCE

*"We cannot choose the things that will happen to us.
But we can choose the attitude we will take toward
anything that happens. Success or failure depends on
your attitude."*

-- Alfred A. Montapert

Workplace violence is a complex subject. It has become a major problem for organizations and is a subject that raises more questions than there are answers. This makes finding solutions to the problem nearly impossible.

To date, no piece of research has provided a clear reason that will explain why violence occurs in one workplace setting and not another. We do know, however, that no workplace is immune. History has shown that workplace violence can happen anywhere. Accepting the fact that literally everyone comes into and leaves the workplace with some sort of "baggage," will go a long way toward under- standing the nature of the problem.

Stressful situations and the emotions that are often created by them are not something that can be easily "checked" at the factory or office door. Generally, if we are unhappy in our job, that unhappiness will follow us out the door and into our relationship with family and friends. A bad day at work usually means a bad day at home. The converse is also true.

Being unhappy at home will usually follow us out the door and into the workplace. Once it enters the work setting, that unhappiness will likely have an effect on everyone with whom we come into contact, our supervisors, co-workers and our attitude toward the job we perform. The result is often unsatisfactory performance, inferior quality, poor service and the likelihood of a disciplinary situation.

As our internal value system is touched and threatened and our feelings negatively impacted, we become candidates for having a truly bad day. How employees approach their fellow workers during these emotionally charged periods may make the difference between having peace and tranquility in the workplace or adding more fuel to an already enraging fire. Without proper training, most supervisors, managers and employees are ill-equipped and unprepared to deal with the emotional needs of the employees they work with and supervise.

It is a fact, workplace violence does not just happen. There are always signs, usually detectable before the incident, but often ignored or inadequately addressed either at home or at the job site. These missed signs can become the basis for disaster. The employer who learns to recognize the early signs, personal problems and stresses created by the workplace will usually make a difference in the de-escalation of a potentially violent situation. Such things as terminations, layoffs, poor performance evaluations, demotion and employee discipline are all issues that incite and instigate the anger that oftentimes turns into rage and then becomes violence.

Awareness and education are the keys that unlock the box for understanding workplace problems. Improving communications, recognizing the early warning signs of erratic or changed employee behavior and learning to deal with that behavior through well developed programs that are fairly and consistently applied in a balanced discipline system will go a long way toward bringing peace and harmony into the workplace.

Conflict Resolution
"What your mind possesses your body expresses."
                                                              --Anonymous

Every workplace is a hot bed of emotions and conflict which can easily erupt into a confrontational setting. What can an employer do to lessen the tensions that arise in the workplace? Learning to deal with conflict in the proper manner may be the only answer. So how does this internal conflict arise? The causes often arise from the diversity of the workplace and the natural stress that exists within it. While no two situations are alike, there is usually a common theme. Each situation will have its own unique set of characteristics, some more prone to tension than others, and they all need to be addressed.

The fastest way to get to the root of the problem is for the employer to develop training for its employees, supervisors and managers through programs that are directed toward the settlement of employee differences. Teaching employees how to communicate with each other and developing a culture that encourages calmness, not adversity, will go a long way toward creating a peaceful work environment.

Handling Confrontation

"I am not arguing with you, I am telling you."

-- J. McN.Whistler

The job assignment most supervisors and managers find both unpleasant and intimidating is the thought that they must be confrontational with the employees they supervise. Clearly confrontation is something most people wish to avoid. The thought of having to tell someone something that might result in open hostility, angry debate or threats of violence creates a lot of anxiety. But confrontation, when done properly, can add an element of cooperation and respect among the work force.

The ability to confront an individual hinges on the ability to separate the person from the problem. A supervisor or manager must learn the correct way to address a work issue while at the same time paying attention to the individual. Understanding that, for most people, work is their life and that losing a job can be a very traumatic and stressful experience will go a long way toward problem resolution. How employers deal with this emotionally charged issue is a critical part of the process necessary for diffusion of a crisis.

Employers should always approach the confrontation process with a positive attitude. Remember, the purpose of the confrontation is to calm, correct and help the person. Despite the cloud of fear that often surrounds this process, confrontation must be carried out in a positive manner, avoiding the negatives if possible. Confrontation, when handled properly, sends the message that the supervisor or manager is concerned and wants to help the employee work things out.

Throughout the confrontation process, the supervisor or manager must keep in mind that there is a difference between what constitutes confrontation and what is criticism. Confrontation, if approached properly, will likely establish cooperation while criticism, on the other hand, even with the best of intentions usually leaves the person feeling unattached or less than adequate.

The ability to effectively confront a person focuses on the ability to separate the person from the problem, a delicate but necessary balance. When a manager or supervisor can confront the problem and still pay attention to the employee he/she will be in a better position to deliver their message i.e. "I am concerned about this issue but more importantly I am concerned about you, let's work on this together." Criticism, on the other hand, will have the opposite effect. It is often delivered with little regard for the person. Supervisor and manager must learn to engage, not enrage.

If confrontation is going to be effective, it must take on the form of encouragement and cooperation. It must become a positive experience. Change, which is usually the goal of confrontation, must be encouraging not discouraging. So how does one approach the confrontation process? -- very carefully and with a positive attitude. Remember, it is not criticism the supervisor or manager is seeking to accomplish. In this process, the supervisor or manager must never lose sight of the real purpose for the confrontation. They are there to help the person correct a problem or situation.

The supervisor or manager must also avoid commingling his motives and intentions and should always work toward gaining cooperation. In a nutshell, confrontation is nothing more than a glorified form of encouragement. The smart manager or supervisor always wants the confrontation to be positive. While confrontation may not be the most pleasant thing in the world to do, it can become a positive experience if properly carried out.

This is not going to be easy, so take a deep breath, exhale and let the process begin. Here are a few rules that will help:

- *Always be honest, but do not beat around the bush:* Do not lie, misrepresent or distort the truth to save feelings. Face the uncomfortable situation and come straight to the point. Approach the problem with a pleasant but persistent attitude. Avoid hesitation or talking about the weather, it will not help. Get to the issue at hand.

- *Always take the initiative:* Be straightforward and assertive about the reason for meeting with the person and make an honest effort to resolve the problem together. Stay within yourself, always focused and controlled. The problem is real and it is there in front of you. It will not go away until you deal with it directly. Procrastination will only make matters worse.

- *Always time your approach:* Try to approach the person within a reasonable time after the problem has arisen. If you are upset or angry because of the other person's behavior, delay the confrontation until such time that you have control of your emotions (usually the next day). Attacking a problem while your emotions are high will only compound the problem. You must always be in control of your emotions before you attempt to confront those of the employee with whom you will be dealing.

- *Always say what you mean and mean what you say:* If you cannot support it, do not say it. Anger in your voice or mannerisms is easily seen by the other party and creates unrealistic demands which you will not be able to support. A good rule of thumb, "always be cool and in control." You will impress some and astonish others.

- *Always have compassion and remember to act human:*
  Be yourself, keep your emotions under control and stay
  focused on your purpose for being there, to assist and
  help a fellow human being. Being unemotional, uncar-
  ing and difficult is not the right plan of action. It is also
  not wrong to move from the business at hand to a
  personal note when the situation dictates. Some things
  do not have to be perfect and when it is all done, say
  "thank you." To be fair, firm and forgiving is to be
  human, it is not a sign of weakness. Jim Valvano once
  said, "My players need me more when they lose than
  when they win." Remember, when the great help the
  small, both become just the right size.

One final point, nothing will reduce your credibility as a
supervisor or manager faster than your unwillingness to
address an obvious employee problem. Directly confronting
the source of the conflict will go a long way toward creating
a positive work environment.

Handling Terminations
*"Keep in mind that the true meaning of an individual is how
he treats a person who can do him absolutely no good."*
-- Ann Landers

As earlier noted, for many people work is a way of life and
their job is a very important part of that life. When approach-
ing any aspect of job loss, one must do so by remembering
the same guidelines that have been suggested in dealing with
the confrontation process. The threat of a job loss raises the
employee's emotional bar to the next level. For the affected
employee, it is a moment filled with crisis and must therefore
be approached in an honest, sincere and straight-forward

manner. The supervisor or manager should always plan their approach, seek to minimize humiliation and begin the process with an element of caution. The goal is to prevent employee stress and the anger that is usually associated with the prospect of losing one's job. By controlling stress and anger, the supervisor or manager may also be able to prevent an incident of workplace violence from occurring. Listed below are some guidelines that the supervisor or manager should find helpful in their approach to dealing with this problem.

1) Recognize that an employee's failure may also be the employer's failure. The supervisor or manager must do all he can throughout the employment process to assist the employee with his/her growth and development in the organization.

2) Maintain an honest appraisal system at all levels in the organization. Whether you put it in writing or state it orally, make sure the appraisal system that is used is fair and consistently applied. Everyone needs to know how they are doing. Honesty throughout the appraisal process is essential.

3) Document, document, document. Give everyone a chance to improve by discussing the good, bad and ugly aspects of their job performance. Confronting poor performance is probably the toughest responsibility for a supervisor or manager to carry out. However, not doing anything is worse. So tell your employees how they are doing, put it in writing and follow-up all poor performance evaluations.

4) If an employee's unsatisfactory job performance continues, confront the employee (remember the rules). Put the facts on the line. If an employee is performing poorly, do not wait until the next

annual review. Tell them now - never let job failure or poor performance be a surprise. Warn if appropriate - act when necessary.

5) Always attempt to properly time your job actions and have a business reason for what you are doing. A job loss following a successful performance review is often difficult to understand and accept.

6) When dealing with job reductions consider alternative methods such as retraining or job relocation within the organization.

7) When the job reduction or loss is the only alternative, attempt to give as much advance notice to the employee as possible. If there is a company policy or collective bargaining agreement in place, follow it. If outplacement is an option then the employer should be advised to seriously consider it.

8) Always act within the requirements of the law whenever you are dealing with any employee displacement issue. There should always be a business reason for your decision and never base your job actions on a discriminatory motive. If the individuals impacted by the job loss or termination are in a protected class because of their age, sex, race or disability, the employer should consider consulting with qualified legal counsel before the job action takes place. This will be viewed as a wise investment of your resources.

9) Plan every termination meeting. Know who will conduct the meeting and their agenda. Will counseling be necessary? Outplacement? What about benefits, separation allowances and other related unemployment issues?

10) If outplacement counseling is available, plan and develop the program in advance. Assist the af-

fected employees in the counseling process. Consider having the outplacement agency on site to provide instant counseling to the affected employee or group.

11)   Train your supervisors and managers and let them know in advance what is happening and why. Counsel them with prepared scripts if necessary on what to say and what not to say.

12)   During the actual termination/separation meeting, be diplomatic in your approach, control your emotions and remember to be sympathetic and understanding. Also try to keep the meeting short, to the point and non-confrontational.

13)   During the termination meeting, have empathy and always be considerate of the feelings of the employees whose jobs are being affected. Do not be degrading or condescending in your approach. Explain the business basis for the company's decision, acknowledge the employee's contributions to the organization and thank them for their efforts.

14)   If a severance arrangement is part of the separation package, be generous. How the monetary plan will be developed is a matter that should be dealt with on a case-by-case basis. Whatever you do, be fair and consistent with the application of any severance package. Discipline yourself to put it in writing and explain the program to each affected employee.

15)   Will medical benefits be continued and for how long? Will access to an Employee Assistance Program be available to the employees following their employment separation. If so, be prepared to explain the process. Also remember your obliga-

tions under the Consolidated Omnibus Budget Reconciliation Act of 1985 (COBRA) as they relate to benefit continuation.

16)   When the explaining is over, allow the employees to leave the premises with their confidence and dignity intact. Except in the most difficult of termination situations, avoid escorting employees from the premises. After the employees turn in their keys, credit cards, etc., allow them to leave the premises on their own terms. You may want to consider a policy that allows these employees to return to the premises for their personal items at a later time and after hours.

17)   Following the employment separation, have qualified staff available, usually a representative from the Human Resources Department, to answer employee questions. Avoid giving bad references. This may have legal implications.

18)   If there is a negative reaction to the employment separation action including threats or other violent responses, take them seriously and consult with your management team and local law enforcement. Never return threatening comments, threats or behavior. Learn to control your emotions and attempt to disarm by listening and being empathic.

Showing compassion to employees at the time of an employment separation and by controlling your emotions, the employer representative will likely reduce the risk of a violent action occurring. Remember, when the employees sense you are being objective, they will perceive you as being honest. Proper planning of the situation and leaving nothing to chance is sound advice. Always react rationally. When you treat people fairly and honestly, they will usually respond in like fashion.

Some Thoughts About Outplacement
"No act of kindness, no matter how small, is ever wasted."
                                                                --AESOP

Once a fashionable buzzword referred to as a "luxury" in the employment process, outplacement has now become a necessity for both the employer and employee. The outplacement process is designed to prepare the displaced employee for the difficult task of finding new employment.

Outplacement is often a customized and comprehensive program designed to develop new career opportunities by relocating the separated employee into the proper job assignment as promptly as possible. It has been defined as a termination or employment separation benefit designed to ease and accelerate the outplaced employee's transition to a new job opportunity or employment relationship.

Having an outplacement plan may also help reduce the stress often associated with the loss brought about by downsizing or a reduction in force. Outplacement programs are usually conducted individually or in group counseling by a qualified professional, who may be a behavioral therapist or executive counselor. During the outplacement educational process, individuals are provided a work setting with a telephone and computer where they learn to create and disseminate their resume and begin the job search process. Video-taped practice interviews, usually followed by counselor evaluation, may also be part of the process.

When outplacement programs are in place they usually begin immediately following an employee's notification of job loss. The programs vary, and a company may have different levels tailored to meet the needs of the sponsoring employer and affected employee. Generally, each level of the outplacement process is designed to restore the displaced individual's self-esteem following the job loss and to develop the new job seeker into a top-flight job candidate.

Properly developed and extended programs created by a responsible outplacement company will have the effect of helping the individual cope with the reality of job loss. It will also prepare the employee for the task of a job search by assisting them in developing the tools needed to properly plan the search, as well as the organization and implementation of that plan. While all of this is being done, the individual's self-esteem is being slowly restored and the levels of stress and humiliation which usually follow the announcement of the job loss are lessened.

Counseling Hints for Supervisors and Managers
"If you are patient in one moment of anger, you will escape a hundred days of sorrow."
-- Ancient Chinese Saying

The job of managing, particularly as it relates to supervisors and managers, plays a big part in controlling and diminishing the likelihood of a violent act occurring in your workplace. In their capacity as a supervisor or manager, it is their job to coach, encourage, offer support and resolve work-related problems in order to improve productivity and service. The supervisor or manager is the chosen leader designated to help develop the skills of employees. Although the supervisor or manager cannot control the behavior of employees, he/she is in a position to influence and affect their behavior.

While the supervisor or manager has not been placed into the workplace as a counselor, they nonetheless can have a profound effect on the employees they supervise. What they say and do can seriously affect a person's well-being.

A common dilemma found among this management group is the ability to achieve a balance for dealing with an individual's on-the-job problems without interfering or intruding into the personal life of the employees they supervise. Not an easy task, especially as it relates to the many personal problems that are brought into the workplace, all of which affect an individual's job performance and the work environment. Here are some helpful hints that may help the supervisor or manager deal with an employee's job-related problems.

- Do not sit in judgment.
- Never ridicule or belittle the problem but be sympathetic and understanding.
- Avoid giving advice unless requested to do so; however, before doing so, make sure you get all the facts.
- Be a listener not a talker. Remember it is the employee who has the problem. Be sure to hear the employee out, let them tell their story and do not interrupt.
- When you are listening, learn to listen more.
- Maintain employee confidences. Remember that they opened up and shared their problems with you.
- When seeking a solution, always try to find one that is best for the situation.
- When discussing the employee's problem, be sure to make eye contact and show them that you care and are an interested listener.
- After hearing the employee's story, ask "What do you think you should do?" This will help you to understand their reason for seeking advice.
- Define the problem. What needs fixing? Avoid labeling the employee's problem. Reframe the problem to make sure you understand it.

- Let the employee talk. This may allow the employee to come up with his/her own options.
- Never support changing what cannot be changed.
- Be objective throughout the counseling/listening process.
- It is important to know your limitations. If the problem is beyond your expertise, do not be afraid to tell the person and direct them to another source (i.e. the Human Resource Department, an Employee Assistance Program, other counseling, etc.).

Learning to be helpful in the counseling process is nothing more than patiently bearing witness and being there for the other person. If the employee you are counseling believes you are sincere and objective, you will be perceived as being honest. When an employee knows you care, the employee will also care, and that will go a long way toward making a difference in achieving a positive resolution of the problem.

CHAPTER EIGHT

MANAGING DIVERSITY -
DEALING WITH THE CHANGING WORKPLACE

"Do not think of today's failures, but of the success that may come tomorrow. You have set yourself a difficult task, but you will succeed if you persevere; and you will find a joy in overcoming the obstacles."
--Helen Keller

Over the years employers and their respective management teams have remodeled, renovated, reorganized, restructured and to some extent revolutionized every aspect of their business operations in an attempt to make it a more effective entity. When the economy was booming that is what was expected. During prosperous times these things were taken for granted. A wide-open marketplace meant a little less quality and workmanship (everybody is doing it), sales were up and the rules of discipline in the workplace were often softened.

Somewhere along the way, in the midst of all this success, the priorities of the business world became misaligned. Then the economy slowed and the bubble burst. Recession, job reductions, and unemployment became the new buzzwords. In the middle of all these changes, corporate compliance began to disappear, markets tightened and competition became more fierce. So what did management do? It decided that in order to meet these new challenges it had to tighten its belt and start taking things back. The pressure was now placed squarely on the shoulders of the organization in order for it to survive.

As a result of this activity, there was a physical and emotional change occurring in the workplace. Technological advances, a mobile society combined with a mixture of cultures, personalities and age groups were now making up a very different workforce. The workplace has become a mixture of foreign workers from around the world, some who may not speak English very well. There are also American workers with pink hair, dreadlocks, multiple tattoos and more body piercing than you have fingers. Are these differences between the generations real and what is management doing about it? The answer to this question is "YES" and management seems to be doing very little about it.

The workplace, once filled with employees who had money and financial security as their priority, (the "do it because it's part of the job and get paid for it" generation), is now being supplemented and in some instances replaced by a generation of workers who easily adapt to change, enjoy working in teams but show less respect for the establishment. The net effect of these changes is that the workplace has become more formal and insensitive and the changes were being felt by the employees. Yet the needs of the employees did not seem to change. The employee's desire to be treated with respect and dignity, remained a high priority.

How an employer approaches the management of workplace diversity and how the employer learns to control the differences created by the different generation groups will go along way towards lessening workplace problems. Clearly, management must learn to manage diversity within its organization in order to reduce the stress, anger and violence that is naturally created by combining different work groups. Management must also learn to control the setting in which these employees work. In a fast changing economy, success-ful job performance can no longer be taken for granted. It has become a condition of employment, not an optional consider-ation.

Listed below are some interesting generalizations that have been made about the different generation groups:

Silent Generation:
- 54-71 years old
- Hard working
- Economically conscious and trusting
- Generally optimistic about the future
- Strong set of moral obligations
- Follow the rules of the workplace

Boomer Generation:
- 35-53 years old
- Strong set of ideas and traditions
- Family oriented
- Fearful of the future
- Politically conservative and socially liberal

Generation X:
- 15-34 years old
- Like to live in the present and experiment
- Look for immediate results
- Selfish and cynical
- Depend on parents
- Questions authority
- Look to foster pride in the workplace
- Crave immediate rewards and recognition
- Feel they are carrying the burden of the previous generation

Generation Y:
- 14 and younger
- Very materialistic, selfish and disrespectful
- Technologically literate
- Growing up fast but without good role models
- Adapt easily to change
- Enjoy working in teams
- Innovative
- Willing to implement new systems and ideas

Common Features in Generations X and Y:
- Raised by television
- Grew up without both biological parents in the home
- Witness to divorce or separation of their parents
- Generally grew up with no one at home after school
- Pessimistic about the future
- Very dependent on their parents
- More likely to challenge rationale behind rules and policies in the workplace
- Likely to ignore direct commands
- Less likely to adhere to established dress codes
- More receptive to flexible scheduling

Those in the workplace who once accepted the rules and policies of the organization as being part of their job, now challenge the rules or ignore them totally. Pay alone does not seem to be the answer because it does not keep them happy. So what should the employer do? The answer may be as simple as changing the way it deals with the problems of the workplace and recognizing that the needs of those who need to be managed have changed.

A recent Conference Board survey reported that there are an increasing number of American workers of all ages and income levels who were unhappy in their jobs. There was a widespread feeling noticed that jobs are not providing the satisfaction that they once did. This should make all employers sit up, listen and be concerned. The employees are sending a clear message to their employers that company bonus plans, promotional policies and educational training programs are no longer the satisfying elements of the job. The irony of this report is that the least satisfied group, ages 35 to 44, was the "happiest group" in a prior survey.

Managing workplace diversity is not a simple one-time task but an every day challenge. It has been said that: "Managing diversity is about managing people who aren't like you and who don't necessarily aspire to be like you. ... It means building systems and a culture that unite different people in common pursuit without undermining their diversity ... We must take differences into account while developing a cohesive whole." (R. Roosevelt Thomas, Jr., Managing Diversity, Moorehouse College).

Clearly, the employer of today can no longer say, "This is the way we're going to do it and that's it." The threat of firing employees to get them to follow the rules is fast losing its effectiveness. This "new" generation of employees will say, like the words of the song, "Take this job and shove it" and then will quickly march off to the nearest state or federal agency to file a job-related complaint (i.e. National Labor Relations Board, Wage & Hour, OSHA, Civil Rights, etc.).

So how does the employer deal with this latest challenge and what can it do to locate the missing ingredient, that necessary element that the employer must emphasize in the workplace -- humanization of the worker. The answer might be as easy as a re-introduction into the workplace of some basic elements: respect, dignity, courtesy and compassion. In other words, employers must develop a culture that encourages opening and keeping open the lines of communication between all of its employees. The employer must also learn to treat its employees like they would want to be treated and to take a more active role in the effort of reconciling workplace (cultural) differences.

If an employer is unable to relate to the employees with the multiple generation ideals and fails to make a realistic effort to bridge this growing generation gap, it will never establish a good relationship among the employees who compose its workforce. Open communication and management training about employee needs in the workplace must become standard operating procedure. Employee recognition, respect and dignity must replace things like "human resource development" and "employee relations improvement." These buzzwords are often viewed by employees to be without any real meaning or effect. Simply, the employer must create a positive work environment by its actions.

Now is the time for every employer to start practicing what it preaches so that it can position itself to survive in a work setting that seeks equality, communication and cooperation between management and workers. Aren't we all on the same team when it comes to achieving the goals and reducing stress in the workplace?

So, what should employers be doing? Well for starters, they should show their employees that they care. This does not mean becoming best buddies with the workforce, but it does mean that employees should be made to feel good about themselves, their co-workers, supervisors and managers. You like them - they like you, it is that simple, but do not try to fake it.

Employers must create an atmosphere whereby every supervisor or manager in the organization is viewed as important as the other, not necessarily in their authority within the organization's hierarchy but to the employees they are responsible for managing. What every organization should be teaching and preaching is that "it's not about me, it's about us." Every employer should make an honest effort to show its employees that it cares. The rewards, which the employer should not be expecting, will flow naturally. Remember, a positive working relationship with the employees is a productive relationship and a necessary ingredient for creating a less stressful environment. Throughout this process, it is important that every employer and its entire management team become and remain emotionally interested in their employees but *never* emotionally involved with them. To do otherwise may create some very serious problems.

How should employers go about the task of blending the different generations that comprise the workplace into a cohesive and effective team? That remains the ultimate challenge, a challenge that must be accepted and met by every employer, in order for them to succeed.

The place to start is the recognition that managing workplace diversity, like recognizing and dealing with workplace stress and violence, is everyone's responsibility, from the entry level employee to the very top level of management. Managing diversity is an ongoing educational process, one that takes a great deal of time and effort. Employers must become cognizant of the value and belief systems held by their employees. Employers must also be able to recognize stereotypical personalities and to explore the personalities that make up the different generations and diverse groups that make up the workplace.

Every employer, every level of management and every employee must face up to their individual biases and prejudices and be able to tactfully point out the biases of others. Employers must learn to listen and to ask questions without being intrusive. Employers must show concern for their employees and be sincere in that process. Employers must learn to accept and embrace employee differences rather than try to change everything or to make others try to agree to do it "their way or the highway."

Employers can only learn to manage diversity and understand the generational differences of its workforce by understanding that it is everyone's job to reach a cultural comfort zone. Every supervisor and manager must be taught to understand that the employees they supervise are human beings, each with their special set of needs and goals. This is the only way management can hope to successfully coach and counsel them.

Supervisors and managers must also learn to listen to their employees and be willing to give them a few minutes of their undivided attention whenever it is prudent to do so. It is equally important that employees are made to feel that their contributions, both big and small, are not only noticed but respected and appreciated by management. There is an energizing and positive feeling that comes from a sense of belonging, a feeling that you are a part of the organization. This is an important step and a truly motivating aspect of the de-stressing process.

Employees who are made to feel important, that they are part of the organization, will help create a teamwork atmosphere that can only lead to prosperity and success. Teamwork must always be the order of the day. Employers must learn to develop a workplace that discourages employee turnover and job strife, in both union and non-union environments. The creation of workplace harmony will go along way toward minimizing internal conflict and the stress that is often associated with fast-paced production or service-oriented organizations. Being able to effectively communicate with employees remains a key element. Talking to, not at, your employees and letting them know that you really care about them will go a long way toward solidifying the employment relationship.

The organization's mission statement, its business philosophy and vision (or whatever the employer chooses to call it) must emphasize those things that are critical to the success of the organization and necessary for the creation of a positive employee-focused workplace culture. Elements such as respect, dignity, trust, empathy, equality, recognition, growth, equal opportunity and open communication are all essential ingredients that must be blended into every level of an organization.

Every organization should have a dual focus - profitability and its people. Employers must consistently be thinking about their employees and their importance to the success of the enterprise. One cannot exist without the other. In order to achieve this success, the employer must maintain a balance between its financial objectives and how it effectively manages its workforce. When all of these ingredients are blended together, the likelihood of achieving success is enhanced. Throughout this process, employees must be constantly reminded that their contributions, both big and small, are not only noticed but respected and appreciated by the organization.

Employee involvement or participation in the work that is being performed is another critical element. Expand, where it is feasible to do so, the employee's role and responsibility within the organization. The more an employer engages in the informational process with its employees about workplace activities, the more important those employees will feel about the value of their input. Experience has shown that the result of employee involvement is usually better when employees have been included in the decision-making process.

The employer must also make an honest commitment to the safety of its work force, their training (for improvement on the job) and the inclusion of favorable benefits (i.e. employee assistance and wellness programs, tuition assistance, on-site training courses, etc.) Having such programs in place will in the long run pay huge dividends. The rewards for the employer, although none should be expected, will show up in reduced employee turnover, improved quality, increased productivity, reductions in absenteeism and work-related injuries. Remember Mr. Employer, a good relationship with your employees and an understanding of their cultural and generational differences (and needs) will create a healthier, less stressful, and more productive work environment. Isn't that what it's all about?

APPENDIX A

SAMPLE POLICIES AND PROCEDURES
HARASSMENT AND WORKPLACE VIOLENCE

"There are two ways of meeting difficulties: you alter the difficulties or you alter yourself."
-- Ancient Chinese Saying

HARASSMENT POLICY

(Name of Organization) is committed to an employee-friendly work environment in which all individuals are treated with respect and dignity. (Name of Organization) believes that every employee has a right to work in a safe and healthful atmosphere that promotes equality in employment and prohibits all forms of discriminatory practices, including harassment and acts of violence.

Harassment can be based on many factors including: sex, race, color, religion, creed, national origin, citizenship status, age, sexual orientation and physical or mental disability.

Sexual harassment occurs when unwelcome conduct of a sexual nature becomes a condition of an employee's continued employment or creates an intimidating, hostile or offensive working environment. Sexual harassment may include a range of subtle and not so subtle behaviors and may also involve individuals of the same or different gender. Examples of sexual and sex-based harassment include, but are not limited to the following:

- Requests for sexual favors (whether explicit or implicit).
- Unwanted sexual advances or propositions.
- Threats by managers to discipline, discharge or deprive an employee of an existing benefit unless the employee agrees to engage in sexual conduct.
- Demands by managers that an employee engage in sexual conduct in order to get a promotion, raise or some other employment benefit.
- Promises by managers that they will reward an employee with a promotion, raise or some other employment benefit if the employee engages in sexual conduct.
- Any unwelcome touching, patting, pinching, caressing, brushing against another's body or other sexually suggestive physical contacts by managers or co-workers.
- Suggestive comments; sexually oriented jokes; sexually oriented kidding or teasing; comments and questions about sexual attributes or activities; graphic commentary about an individual's body, sexual prowess or sexual deficiencies; foul or obscene language or gestures; display of obscene or sexually suggestive pictures; printed materials, computer communications or objects; indecent exposure; and attempts to invade the sexual privacy of another person by managers or co-workers. (These types of conduct may be harassment regardless of whether it is addressed to a specific employee or a general audience.)
- Active or passive encouragement of harassment by others and the failure to report any harassing conduct that an employee witnesses or is otherwise aware.
- Harassment by customers, workers or other third parties doing business with (Name of Organization), if reported to a manager and nothing is done to stop it.

Harassment of any kind, including threats or acts of workplace violence, are contrary to the organization's goal of providing a safe work and healthful work environment for its employees. Any violation of this policy will not be tolerated. Any employee found to have engaged in harassment or any form of threatening or violent behavior will be subject to disciplinary action, up to and including discharge.

PROCEDURES FOR REPORTING DISCRIMINATORY, THREATENING OR VIOLENT BEHAVIOR

If an employee of (Name of Organization) experiences any job related harassment based on sex, sexual orientation, age, race or any other discriminatory factor specified in the (Name of Organization) Equal Employment Opportunity Policy or believes he/she has been treated in an unlawful manner, including being subjected to threats or acts of violence, he/she must promptly report the incident to his/her supervisor or manager. If an employee believes it would be inappropriate to discuss the matter with his/her supervisor or manager, he/she must report it directly to the Human Resources Department. The employee always has the option of reporting the conduct to the company president if he or she prefers. All complaints will be kept confidential to the maximum extent possible.

(Name of Organization) will not allow anyone to take any adverse action against employees because they have reported or participated in the investigation of a claim of discrimination, harassment or incident of workplace violence. (Name of Organization) will promptly conduct a thorough and impartial investigation of all complaints received, and such investigation, to the extent possible, will be carried out in a confidential manner. Upon the conclusion of its investigation, (Name of Organization) will advise the complaining employee of its findings, including any steps taken to prevent further violation of this policy.

The management of (Name of Organization) is responsible for the administration of this policy. Should any supervisors or managers learn of a violation of this policy, they are expected to take whatever steps are necessary to prevent further harm to the affected employee and must promptly report the conduct to the Human Resources Department or company president, for a full and impartial investigation. Failure to report such conduct will be considered a violation of this policy and will subject the supervisor or manager to disciplinary action, up to and including discharge.

Any employee suspected of engaging in harassing or retaliatory conduct of any kind contrary to the terms of this policy, after reasonable investigation, will be subject to disciplinary action, up to and including discharge.

(Name of Organization) prohibits any form of retaliation against an employee for filing a bona fide complaint under this policy or for assisting in a complaint investigation. However, if after investigating any complaint of harassment, unlawful discrimination or workplace violence (Name of Organization) determines that the complaint is not bona fide or that an employee has provided false information regarding the complaint investigation, disciplinary action will be taken against the individual who filed the complaint or provided the false information.

WORKPLACE VIOLENCE POLICY

In a constantly changing business environment, there are many obstacles that may inhibit the employer's obligation to maintain a safe and healthful workplace. One of the most immediate problems that an organization faces is violent or threatening behavior directed toward employees. Although such incidents in our workplace are rare, on occasion we have had situations arise that require prompt action.

(Name of Organization) recognizes the need to maintain an environment where everyone can work safely and without fear. The (Name of Organization) therefore has adopted a "Zero Tolerance" policy against any words or actions that threaten employees or visitors at any (Name of Organization) location. This includes verbal confrontations and behavior that reasonably causes others to feel unsafe or threatened.

The following policy has been adopted by (Name of Organization) with employee safety and welfare as its sole priority. This policy is intended to eliminate the risk of threats and violence in the workplace.

(Name of Organization) will not tolerate threatening, abusive, intimidating or harassing behavior of any kind; possession or use of firearms or any other weapons; physical attacks on any person; or the intentional destruction of another's personal property, whether during the course of employment or in any area around the workplace.

Any employee who threatens or commits an act of violence or threatens use of a weapon, or engages in intimidating behavior of any kind or manner while on the job or in an area around the workplace will be subject to disciplinary action, up to and including discharge.

HOW TO HANDLE THREATENING
OR VIOLENT WORKPLACE BEHAVIOR

Occasions may arise where an individual becomes a threat to our organization's safety or security. In such instances, employees are asked to cooperate in trying to end these situations as quickly as possible and to promptly remove the offender from the workplace setting. If the situation does not involve you, absent yourself from the scene; do not provide an audience. Promptly notify your supervisor or manager and return to your work area.

Physical contact of any kind, no matter how innocently intended, should always be avoided. When dealing with a hostile person, extreme care should be taken not to make comments which might further provoke the party or be proven later to be inaccurate, and possibly used in a subsequent legal action. Make no attempt to contradict, restrain or physically interfere with an irrational person and promptly contact the Human Resources Department. Leave the situation to a designated company official or local law enforcement.

Reporting Duty

Employees of (Name of Organization) are encouraged to promptly raise any workplace violence or safety concerns with their supervisor or manager and to utilize the Procedures for Reporting Discriminatory Threatening or Violent Behavior to report such incidents.

Any employee with first-hand knowledge of a violent or threatening incident or who believes that an individual is engaging in menacing behavior has an absolute duty to report it in the following manner:

1) All urgent and/or potentially dangerous threats or acts of violence must immediately be reported to the (Police Department whose number is _____ or dial 911).
2) All non-urgent threats should be reported to the employee's supervisor or manager and/or Human Resources Department, who will consult with (the company president, designated corporate executive, etc.)
3) All acts or threats of violence in the workplace will be promptly investigated by the (Police Department and Human Resources Department) in a timely manner. A plan of action will be recommended with regard to the individual responsible for the act or threat.

Recordkeeping and documentation about any incident of workplace violence will be maintained by the Human Resources Department and the employee's immediate supervisor. Every effort will be used to protect the employee's right to privacy. In those instances where other employees are considered at risk or in danger, management, in consultation with the Human Resources Department, will act promptly to convey a warning to the employee(s) involved as well as the local Police Department.

APPENDIX B

RECOGNIZING PERSONALITY DISORDERS

"The mind is its own place, and in itself can make Heaven of Hell and a Hell of Heaven."

-- John Milton

The Diagnostic and Statistical Manual of Mental Disorders describes a personality disorder as an enduring pattern of inner experience and behavior that deviates markedly from the expectations of the individual's culture, is pervasive and inflexible, has an onset in adolescence or early adulthood, is stable over time and leads to distress or impairment.

This reference to the several types of personality disorders are stated in this book because the author believes that there may be a direct connection between an individual's psychological disorder, the developed profile of a person who is prone to commit an act of violence and the violent act itself. In addition, there is a strong belief by the prevention community that understanding the characteristics generally associated with personality disorders are a valuable tool in making a later diagnosis of the problem. It is only through knowledge of the problem and the targeting of key elements associated with this list of described personality disorders that we may be able to intercede with therapeutic interventions related to the characteristics of the person who may be prone to violent activity. This is an important first step in the process of recognizing and responding to a potentially violent situation.

The diagnostic and statistical manual content of schemas in personality disorders as listed in the Manual of Mental Disorders is set forth below:

I.   *Avoidant Personality Disorder*

1)   I am socially inept and socially undesirable in work or social situations.
2)   Other people are potentially critical, indifferent, demeaning or rejecting.
3)   I cannot tolerate unpleasant feelings.
4)   If people get close to me, they will discover the "real" me and reject me.
5)   Being exposed as inferior or inadequate will be intolerable.
6)   I should avoid unpleasant situations at all cost.
7)   If I feel or think something unpleasant, I should try to wipe it out or distract myself-- for example, think of something else, have a drink, take a drug or watch television.
8)   I should avoid situations in which I attract attention or I should be as inconspicuous as possible.
9)   Unpleasant feelings will escalate and get out of control.
10)   If others criticize me, they must be right.
11)   It is better not to do anything than to try something that might fail.
12)   If I don't think about a problem, I don't have to do anything about it.

13) Any signs of tension in a relationship indicate the relationship has gone bad; therefore, I should cut it off.

14) If I ignore a problem, it will go away.

II.   *Dependent Personality Disorder*

1) I am needy and weak.

2) I need somebody around available at all times to help me to carry out what I need to do or in case something bad happens.

3) My helper can be nurturant, supportive and confident -- if he or she wants to be.

4) I am helpless when I'm left on my own.

5) I am basically alone -- unless I can attach myself to a stronger person.

6) The worst possible thing would be to be abandoned.

7) If I am not loved, I will always be unhappy.

8) I must do nothing to offend my supporter or helper.

9) I must be subservient in order to maintain his or her good will.

10) I must maintain access to him or her at all times.

11) I should cultivate as intimate a relationship as possible.

12) I can't make decisions on my own.

13) I can't cope as other people can.

14) I need others to help me make decisions or tell me what to do.

III.   *Passive-Aggressive Personality Disorder*

1)   I am self-sufficient, but I do need others to help me reach my goals.

2)   The only way I can preserve my self-respect is by asserting myself indirectly -- for example, by not carrying out instructions exactly.

3)   I like to be attached to people but I am unwilling to pay the price of being dominated.

4)   Authority figures tend to be intrusive, demanding, interfering and controlling.

5)   I have to resist the domination of authorities but at the same time maintain their approval and acceptance.

6)   Being controlled or dominated by others is intolerable.

7)   I have to do things my own way.

8)   Making deadlines, complying with demands and conforming are direct blows to my pride and self-sufficiency.

9)   If I follow the rules the way people expect, it will inhibit my freedom of action.

10) It is best not to express my anger directly but to show my displeasure by not conforming.

11) I know what's best for me and other people shouldn't tell me what to do.

12) Rules are arbitrary and stifle me.

13) Other people are often too demanding.

14) If I regard people as too bossy, I have a right to disregard their demands.

IV.   *Obsessive-Compulsive Personality Disorder*

1)   I am fully responsible for myself and others.
2)   I have to depend on myself to see that things get done.
3)   Others tend to be too casual, often irresponsible, self-indulgent or incompetent.
4)   It is important to do a perfect job on everything.
5)   I need order, systems and rules in order to get the job done properly.
6)   If I don't have systems, everything will fall apart.
7)   Any flaw or defect of performance may lead to a catastrophe.
8)   It is necessary to stick to the highest standards at all times, or things will fall apart.
9)   I need to be in complete control of my emotions.
10) People should do things my way.
11) If I don't perform at the highest level, I will fail.
12) Flaws, defects or mistakes are intolerable.
13) Details are extremely important.
14) My way of doing things is generally the best say.

V.   *Antisocial Personality Disorder*

1)   I have to look out for myself.
2)   Force or cunning is the best way to get things done.
3)   We live in a jungle and the strong person is the one who survives.
4)   People will get me if I don't get them first.
5)   It is not important to keep promises or honor debts.
6)   Lying and cheating are OK as long as you don't get caught.

7)   I have been unfairly treated and am entitled to get my fair share by whatever means I can.

8)   Other people are weak and deserve to be taken.

9)   If I don't push other people, I will get pushed around.

10)   I should do whatever I can get away with.

11)   What others think of me doesn't really matter.

12)   If I want something, I should do whatever is necessary to get it.

13)   I can get away with things so I don't need to worry about bad consequences.

14)   If people can't take care of themselves, that's their problem.

VI.   *Narcissistic Personality Disorder*

1)   I am a very special person.

2)   Since I am so superior, I am entitled to special treatment and privileges.

3)   I don't have to be bound by the rules that apply to other people.

4)   It is very important to get recognition, praise, and admiration.

5)   If others don't respect my status, they should be punished.

6)   Other people should satisfy my needs.

7)   Other people should recognize how special I am.

8)   It's intolerable if I'm not accorded my due respect or don't get what I'm entitled to.

9)   Other people don't deserve the admiration or riches that they get.

10)   People have no right to criticize me.

11)   No one's needs should interfere with my own.

12) Since I am so talented, people should go out of their way to promote my career.
13) Only people as brilliant as I am understand me.
14) I have every reason to expect grand things.

VII. *Histrionic Personality Disorder*

1) I am an interesting, exciting person.
2) In order to be happy I need other people to pay attention to me.
3) Unless I entertain or impress people, I am nothing.
4) If I don't keep others engaged with me, they won't like me.
5) The way to get what I want is to dazzle or amuse people.
6) If people don't respond very positively to me, they are rotten.
7) It is awful if people ignore me.
8) I should be the center of attention.
9) I don't have to bother to think things through--I can go by my "gut" feeling.
10) If I entertain people, they will not notice my weakness.
11) I cannot tolerate boredom.
12) If I feel like doing something, I should go ahead and do it.
13) People will pay attention only if I act in extreme ways.
14) Feelings and intuition are much more important than rational thinking and planning.

VIII. *Schizoid and Schizotypal Personality Disorders*

1) It doesn't matter what other people think of me.
2) It is important for me to be free and independent of others.
3) I enjoy doing things more by myself than with other people.
4) In many situations, I am better off to be left alone.
5) I am not influenced by others in what I decide to do.
6) Intimate relations with other people are not important to me.
7) I set my own standards and goals for myself.
8) My privacy is much more important to me than closeness to people.
9) What other people think doesn't matter to me.
10) I can manage things on my own, without anybody's help.
11) It's better to be alone than to feel "stuck" with other people.
12) I shouldn't confide in others.
13) I can use other people for my own purposes as long as I don't get involved.
14) Relationships are messy and interfere with freedom.

IX.   *Paranoid Personality Disorder*

1) I cannot trust other people.
2) Other people have hidden motives.
3) Others will try to use me or manipulate me if I don't watch out.
4) I have to be on guard at all times.

5) It isn't safe to confide in other people.

6) If people act friendly, they may be trying to use or exploit me.

7) People will take advantage of me if I give them the chance.

8) For the most part, other people are unfriendly.

9) Other people will deliberately try to demean me.

10) Often people will deliberately want to annoy me.

11) I will be in serious trouble if I let other people think they can get away with mistreating me.

12) If other people find out things about me, they will use them against me.

13) People often say one thing and mean something else.

14) A person whom I am close to could be disloyal or unfaithful.

REFERENCES BIBLIOGRAPHY

American Psychiatric Association. Diagnostic and Statistical Manual of Mental Disorders, Fourth Edition, Washington, D.C., 1994.

Baron, S. Anthony, Ph.D. Violence in the Workplace, a Prevention and Management Guide for Businesses, Pathfinder Publishing of California, 1993.

BNA. Daily Labor Report, August 22, 2002.

BNA. Human Resources Report, September 9, 2002.

Brenaer, John and Betsy Summerfield. Building a Workplace Violence Plan, VCCA Journal, Vol. 10, Summer 1996.

Cassidy, Susan O. Edited by Alain J. Courturier, MD, MS, Legal Challenges, Occupational and Environmental Infectious Diseases, OEM Press, 2000.

Cowley, Geoffrey. Our Bodies, Our Fears, Newsweek, February 24, 2003.

Department of Health and Human Services, Centers for Disease Control and Prevention, National Institute for Occupational Safety and Health (NIOSH).
• NIOSH Facts Bulletin, June 1997.

104   Robert F. Conte

- NIOSH Update, NIOSH Urges Immediate Action to Prevent Workplace Violence, October 1993.
- Request for Assistance in Preventing Homicide in the Workplace, Publication No. 93-109, September 1993.
- Stress ... at Work, Publication No. 99-101, January 1999.
- Violence, Occupational Hazards in Hospitals, Publication No. 2002-101, April 2002.
- Violence in the Workplace, Risk Factors and Prevention Strategies, Publication No. 96-100, June 1996.

Frank, William S. 25 Ways to Prevent Workplace Violence During Terminations, the Human Resources Zone, July 24, 2000.

Good Stuff. Progressive Business Collections, 2000.

Grossman, Robert J. Bulletproof Practices (For Dealing with Workplace Violence), HR Magazine, November 2002.

Hirsch, Jeffrey L., Esq. Workplace Violence, Occupational Safety and Health Handbook, An Employer Guide to OSHA Laws, Regulations and Practices, Second Edition, Lexis Law Publishing®, 1999.

Johnson, Mike. Workplace Violence, Tribune Business Weekly, October 7, 2002.

Keeton, W., R. Dobbs, R. Keeton and D. Owens. Prosser and Keeton on the Law of Torts, (5th Ed., 1984).

Kolenda, Mike K., Ph.D. and Jill Soens, MS. Employee Stress: What Supervisors Can Do! Executive Journal, April 1989.

Levin, Robert L., Esq. Workplace Violence: Navigating through the Minefield of Legal Liability, The Labor Lawyer, Vol. 11, No. 2, Summer 1995.

Logan, Tim. Echoes of Violence - Scars and Memories, South Bend Tribune, December 8, 2002.

McDermott, Brian L., Esq. Violence in the Workplace: An Unfortunate Reality, The Workplace Lawyer, Indiana State Bar Association, Fall 2002.

McGoey, Chris E., CPP, CSP, CAM. The Crime Doctor™. Workplace Violence at the Office.

Minor, Marianne. Preventing Workplace Violence, Positive Management Strategies, CRISP Publications, Inc., 1995.

OSHA Fact Sheet. Workplace Violence.
• U.S. Department of Labor, Occupational Safety and Health Administration, 2002.

OSHA Voluntary Guidelines on Preventing Workplace Violence, The Bureau of National Affairs, Inc., 1996.

Pocket Pal™ Diary, Myron Manufacturing Corporation, 2000 and 2001.

Scott, N. "Stress Has Become the New Buzzword," South Bend Tribune, August 27, 1988.

The Associated Press News Release, as reported in The South Bend Tribune on July 9, 10 and 12, 2003.

The Pocket Book of Quotations, A Cardinal Edition, Pocket Books, Inc., New York, 5th Printing, 1953.

The Ultimate Pocket Positives, The Five Mile Press, Noble Park Victoria, Australia, 2001.

White, Darcelle D. Dr., Dr. Linda M. Kinzckowski, Dr. Pamela Speelman, and Martha J. Obijnyk. Is Domestic Violence About to Spill into Your Client's Workplace? Michigan Bar Journal, October 2002.

Winning Words, complied by Allen Klein, Portland House, an imprint of Random House Value Publishing, Inc., New York, N.Y., 2002.

Workplace Violence, Human Resources Office, Woods Hole Oceanographic Institution.

Workplace Violence Prevention and Response, University of California, Irvine.